(Ir)responsible

TORN CURTAIN PUBLISHING
Auckland, New Zealand
www.torncurtainpublishing.com

ISBN Softcover 978-1-991299-46-8
ISBN EPub 978-1-991299-47-5

Cover art by Birmingham Museum Trust (unsplash.com). William Morris, Honeysuckle, 1896. Used with permission.

Typeset in Millar Banner, Yeseva One, and Raleway.

Cataloguing in Publishing Data

Title: (Ir)responsible: Living true to the call but free from the burden
Author: Rebecca Green
Subjects: Work-life balance, mental health, Christian ministry and leadership, inspirational, self-help, spiritual growth, personal growth, pastoral resources.

A copy of this title is held at the National Library of New Zealand.

(Ir)responsible

LIVING TRUE TO THE CALL BUT
FREE FROM THE BURDEN

REBECCA GREEN

To my church family

Then Jesus said, "Come to me, all of you who are weary and carry heavy burdens, and I will give you rest. Take my yoke upon you. Let me teach you, because I am humble and gentle at heart, and you will find rest for your souls. For my yoke is easy to bear, and the burden I give you is light."

Matthew 11:28-30

Contents

To the Reader

Dear Friend,

Firstly, welcome. I pray this space becomes a place of refreshing and freedom. Throughout these pages I am going to share my personal experience of grappling with the weight of responsibility, how for many years I felt trapped by expectations, and how I finally came up for air. I'm going to be real, and I am going to be honest. Sometimes I'm even going to share out of my prayer journal. But let's just make a deal right here, at the beginning: No judging! I won't judge you and you don't judge me. We will journey together, unpack together, and then we will redesign life together.

I am writing the book I wish I could have read at age ten, but also at age thirty-nine and every year in between. As a wife, mum, friend and pastor, there have been moments when my life has been so busy, full, chaotic and heavy that I have felt like I have been teetering on the edge of a cliff. Any small thing could push me over and send me sinking under the waves beneath. I've spent years digging my toes in, fearful of what someone might ask me to do next. But teetering on the brink of survival is not how God intended me to live. He never intended for us to shoulder responsibilities alone.

Matthew 11 teaches us that Jesus' yoke is easy and his burden is light, but it wasn't easy for me to begin living that reality. Instead, I lived most of my life under the constant and burdensome narrative that *I am responsible for everything.* That is an exhausting way to live—take it from one who knows!

Perhaps you too have become convinced that you *have to* do it all. Maybe the circumstances of your childhood caused you to grow up more quickly than you should have. Perhaps there was a practical need within your family that, in a difficult season, prompted you to pick up the lion's share of responsibility, and now you can't quite put it down. Maybe stepping into motherhood has been the catalyst for you, taking care of everyone except yourself—you just want to be a good mum, after all. Perhaps, like me, you are in pastoral ministry, and it requires a lot from you—it's hard not to get swallowed up by it all.

If any of that resonates with you, then you are in good company. I see you. I know the weight. I understand. And friend, my prayer is that, as you read this book, God will reveal to you the places that leave you feeling weighed down. As you read my story you might recognise areas in your own life where you have assumed responsibility for holding it all together—beyond what was intended for you. There may be times when you have struggled to share your pain or ask for help in seasons when you *needed* someone to share the load.

I have found on my path that some situations took a bit of unpacking, and sometimes it was painful. Realising hard truths about yourself isn't always easy. But I knew I couldn't maintain that level of responsibility forever. Something had to change about the way I thought about myself—the way I approached everything! I knew that if it didn't, I was risking all the things that meant the most to me. I was risking being the wife to my husband and the mother to our children that I knew they deserved. I was risking every dream I had held onto and every promise I had believed God for. I was even risking the greater calling on my life—I needed to find a better way.

This is not a book about burnout, and it is also not about boundaries. It won't simply be about how to say no. Instead, we are going to talk about how to design our lives so that we can say yes—yes to all that God is calling us to . . . without the fear of going under.

As you read this book, my prayer is that you would experience the same freedom I have.

With love,
Becs
xx

1

Slipping Beneath the Surface

"It wouldn't take much to drown me."

WE WERE A GROUP OF FRIENDS, ALL OF US CHURCH LEADERS, sitting around a living room, coffee cups in hand, each of us talking about the ups and downs of life and ministry, celebrating our triumphs and exposing our struggles. It was a moment of 'real'—honest and brave. As one woman summed up where she was at, she spoke the words, "It wouldn't take much to drown me."

While my friends continued to share and listen to one another, my mind remained stuck on that sentence. The words swirled around inside my head. I picked up my journal and wrote them down. *It wouldn't take much to drown me.* That phrase hit awfully close to home. I had partly stopped listening to what the group was saying as I became confronted by all the different times I had felt threatened by the waves around me. It was as though my friend was putting into words what had been happening in my own life.

That drowning feeling was all too familiar. Life's pressures, responsibilities, to-dos and task lists mounting and piling up faster than I could tick them off. I was only just keeping my head above water. It was the feeling of sinking, of being under the weight of something almost unbearable, and if any small wave, any extra pressure or unexpected thing were to come my way, I would go under.

It wasn't the first time I'd experienced the sensation of drowning. As a child, just a year after my family had moved from England to New Zealand, we had family from back home to visit. We took them to see one of the most popular tourist spots in the country. The motel where we stayed had a great space for kids to play, with trampolines, playgrounds, and a swimming pool. Being in the late eighties, health and safety expectations and compliance were significantly different from what they are today. Around the pool ran a low fence—so low that it was easy for four-year-old me to step right over it. The pool had a black cover lying over the top, and while my older brother and sister were jumping on the trampolines with some neighbouring kids I went wandering around the pool. Without realising that the pool cover was not a solid platform I stepped out onto it and immediately sank underneath, disappearing below the black cover. I don't have many memories from that age, but I do remember this moment. I can recall the confusion as I slipped beneath what I thought was firm ground. But it was the awareness that I was trapped that was the most terrifying. My arms and legs were going a million miles an hour trying to bring myself to the surface so that I could catch a breath, only to realise there was no room for me to gasp for air. Panic quickly set in. One of the boys playing next to my siblings saw me sinking and yelled, "Hey, your sister just went into the pool!" My quick-thinking sister reached over the edge, grabbed me by the hair and held my head out of the water while my brother raced to alert my parents. I was water-logged and mildly traumatised, but I was safe.

You may not have experienced a physical near-drowning but I'm sure you can relate to that feeling in some area of your life. I am wondering if, like me, you know what it's like to slowly sink under. To slowly sink under the weight of all the things you said yes to—but wished you hadn't. All the things you said yes to because you thought you couldn't say no to *All. The. Things.*

Or perhaps you have mastered the art of keeping your eyes and nose just above water, enough to catch a breath and keep on going, your legs frantically circling to hold you afloat. But then, out of nowhere, an unexpected wave surges in and you can no longer hold yourself up. You are suddenly flailing under the water. That unforeseen crisis, job redundancy, mounting pressure in business, relational conflict, weighty leadership decision, difficult meeting—those life twists and turns that pull you under.

I always laugh at one of comedian Jim Gaffigan's stand-up jokes: "You know what it's like having a fourth kid? Imagine you're drowning, then someone hands you a baby." I laugh but I am all too familiar with the reality of that scenario. I may not have four kids but boy—the sentiment resonates. One Saturday afternoon I was sitting on our bed, using our bedroom as a secret hideaway. In all honesty, I think I was trying to escape from more than just the chaos of two boys, a dog and a husband all squashed into a tiny eighty-five-square-metre house. I had a lot on my to-do list and the deadlines were looming, the events on my calendar were many, I had meetings crammed into an already full schedule, and one of our staff had just sent me a text asking if she could meet with me.

The walls of our tiny home seemed like they were closing in. I was struggling to even respond to the latest meeting request. I felt nervous just thinking about what they might want to talk to me about. The more I tried to figure it out, the more anxious I became. There was a heaviness in my chest, and it was becoming hard to get the air I needed to breathe easily. I could feel the strain in my neck and throat as I tried with everything in me to hold it together. Then came a knock at our bedroom door. My husband popped his head in to let me know that we had some unexpected visitors. That was the last thing I needed! The panic took over and I crumbled, my lungs were heaving as I fought to catch my breath. My poor husband didn't know what he had walked into—his usually well-put-together wife was losing her marbles at the drop of a hat. He helped me to find my normal breathing rhythms again before leaving the room to let our guests know I wasn't feeling well and wouldn't be able to join them. I felt so silly that the thought of visitors popping in was too much for me to bear, but at least I understood what was happening to me . . . because this wasn't my first panic attack.

Living on the Edge

I was in my mid-thirties with two primary schoolers, and we had just finished our summer holiday. My husband and I were both on church staff, he was full-time, and I was part-time, but only just. School was back, church life was ramping up and we were hitting the ground running. It was only the beginning of the church calendar, and our schedule was already busy. Our days were full with our two active boys, a home to maintain, and many family and ministry commitments. My church responsibilities were growing, and February through to April were our biggest and busiest months. I couldn't envisage life slowing down anytime soon.

As a family, we were at our eldest son's athletics competition. It was a piping hot day, and I should have been enjoying the sunshine and fresh air while watching my boy compete. But I wasn't. I couldn't. I felt agitated and unsettled. It was like my skin was crawling and I wanted to shake my limbs free of it. The only way I can describe it is that I felt 'out of my own skin'. My palms were sweating and all I could do was rub them together or on my legs to get them dry, again and again and again. Sitting was making me feel uneasy, so I made up excuses to walk somewhere: to the bathroom, to the water fountain to fill up my water bottle, to the food truck to find something to eat—anything to distract me from the panic that was welling up inside me. I could almost feel it rising from my stomach, through my chest and then tightening around my throat. There it was again, the fearful feeling of being trapped, of not knowing how or when I was going to be able to catch my breath.

In my mind, I was both numb and terrified. I felt fear, but of what? My life was good. It was full of wonderful things. I was happy. I loved my family, my home, and my church.

A friend turned up on my doorstep that afternoon. Being a paramedic, she somehow seemed to know I was not okay. We sat down with a cup of tea at my dining table, and she held my wringing hands still. As I told her about what was happening in my physical body, she helped me unpack what was simmering just below the surface. She lovingly led me to a place of seeing my life without the 'everything is fine' glasses I liked to wear. The truth was, I was empty. There was nothing left in the tank. I was carrying so many hats and juggling so many balls, that it felt like I didn't have time to breathe.

If my life could be compared to a large field bordering the edge of a cliff then my field needed some fences. I was getting way too close to the edge, pushing life right out to the limits. There was no margin. No margin for error, no margin for emergencies, and no margin for rest. That afternoon, as I sat at my dining table, I felt like I was teetering on the very edge. Just how long would it be until something sent me over?

And yet so many of us live like that, don't we? We fill our lives to the brim because we think it sounds exciting. Our family has some good friends who sold their home, gave up their careers, downsized their possessions, moved their entire life to a small town, and started a blog called *Slow and Simple*. We often joked that with the way Steve and I lived we could have started a competing blog called *Fast and Complicated*. The reality for many of us, me included, is that busyness quickly becomes a badge of honour. We wear it proudly as though it must mean we are very important. If we are always busy then surely it means that we are needed, we are useful, and the things we are busying ourselves with must be *really* significant.

In our busyness, we like to think we are living life to the max. The only problem with this is that it doesn't leave any room for the unexpected. There is no contingency plan for the things we didn't anticipate. We live in that field tired, overwhelmed, stressed, and under pressure. Without margin for the unexpected, we live every day clinging on, hoping something doesn't come and send us over the edge.

In her 2010 TEDx talk, *The Price of Invulnerability*, Brené Brown made the remark, "We stay so busy that the truth of our lives can't catch up." That had been my reality for a very long time. I was oblivious to the condition of my own life. As I sat in my kitchen, I felt utterly drained. The truth of my life had finally caught up with me. I needed to construct some fences in my field. I needed to do some work to establish some space between where I was living my life and where life became too overwhelming. For way too long I had been walking precariously close to the crumbling edge of that cliff.

After my friend's visit that day, I was left questioning myself. *How on earth did I get here? How did living so close to the edge become normal, okay, and even desirable for me?*

"I am capable," I had told myself. "I am the girl with the high capacity who seems to be able to do it all. I am the one people go to when they are melting down. How can it be that I am now the one who is falling to pieces?"

II

The Quest for Perfection

"You are good because God is good."

"**M**EET DAD AT THE FRONT STEPS AT PICK-UP TIME!" I YELLED out the window to my boys as they ran off to their classrooms. Pulling back out into the traffic, I began driving across town to the appointment I had later that morning. I have a terrible sense of direction, so when I stopped at the traffic lights, I picked up my phone and put the address into Google Maps. Right then, I realised I hadn't let my husband, Steve, know about the pick-up arrangements for after school, so I quickly shot him a text message. I knew if I didn't send it then I would forget. As I returned my phone to its holder, I spotted a police car in my wing mirror. *Perfect! Just what I need. Hopefully, they didn't see me using my phone. Anyway, I wasn't technically driving, so surely there is nothing wrong with that!*

I was in a long line of traffic. The light turned green and then red again. When my turn came to go through, I made sure I was on my best behaviour. The police car sat behind me as I passed through another two intersections. *Whew!* I started to relax. *She mustn't have seen me or I would have been pulled over by now.* But before I could finish that thought, I looked into my rear-view mirror and saw the flashing lights. I pulled over, and as the police officer approached my window, I could feel the heat begin to rise in my cheeks.

"Do you know why I pulled you over today?" she asked.

"No, Officer, I don't." A lump formed in my throat—I knew exactly why.

"You were texting while stopped at a traffic light," she said.

"I was just putting my destination into the navigation app," I replied, omitting the part about texting my husband.

"You must have been doing a whole lot more than that. You were distracted for a while."

I froze, willing myself to say something, but no words came out. I just sat there looking at her. The silence between us felt like it went on forever. Finally, she handed over a piece of paper with a fine and demerit points. *Ouch.* As I pulled back into the traffic and continued to drive, I felt sick to my stomach. I had just lied—and to a police officer of all people. My mind was racing. *I'm supposed to be a Christian. What kind of Christian does that make me? Worse—I'm supposed to be a pastor! What kind of pastor does that make me?!*

I felt the embarrassment to my core. It was as though shame itself was tightening around my throat, and there was that familiar anxious feeling heavy on my chest. I called my husband to confess the fine. I couldn't bring myself to confess the lie.

Keeping Secrets

"Do you lie a lot?" my counsellor queried when I disclosed it to him the following week.

"What do you mean?" I asked, a little offended at his line of questioning. Counsellors tend to be annoyingly observant, and mine was particularly good at it.

"Do you have a habit of keeping secrets?" he clarified.

"I don't think so?"

But now I questioned my own answer. I thought I was an open book. I normally shared everything with my husband, and I had a pretty honest relationship with my close friends. I didn't think there was anything in my life worth keeping quiet. Nothing secret-worthy here. At least, I didn't think there was—until he asked the question and my mind went back to a memory from when I was ten years old.

I was eating lunch with a group of friends in the school playground. These were the days when students could order lunches by bringing a coin-filled envelope to school with their name and order scribbled on the outside. The lunch orders were delivered to the classroom in brown paper bags with the student's name on their bag. That day, a girl joined our lunch group, holding one of those lunch bags. Pulling out the items of food, she began sharing them around. Very rarely was I allowed to enjoy the luxury of a special lunch order, and I felt stoked when she handed me a mini pizza. As I bit into it, however, I looked up to see a stern-looking teacher standing in front of me and holding the hand of a very tearful girl. I hadn't thought to ask any questions, but now I realise I probably should have.

If I'd asked "Whose pizza is it?", I would have learnt that I was on the receiving end of stolen goods. My friends and I had just been caught red-handed! It was a lunch order heist, and I was smack bang in the middle of it. Intentional or unintentional, it didn't change the fact that I was in big trouble. I wanted to say, "But it wasn't me." I was clearly in trouble, and once again, I froze. Nothing came out. The teacher told us that we had to go home, write a letter of apology, have it signed by our parents, and pay back the money.

The money was easy to find. All I had to do was search through my dad's work trousers—he always left coins in there, and he was used to us kids taking them! The more difficult issue was getting a signature. That night in my bedroom, I wrote the letter. *That wasn't too hard.* But to get my parents' signature, I was going to have to confess that I had eaten someone's stolen lunch. *No way was that happening.* I wouldn't. I couldn't.

The next day, I took my one-dollar coin and my unsigned letter, and handed them to the teacher, praying she wouldn't notice the missing signature. Thankfully, she didn't say anything, and neither did I. I'd got away with it!

But now, sitting in my counsellor's office, the memory of that day made me realise that I hadn't suddenly started lying at the age of thirty-six. I had been using secrecy as a way of protecting myself since I was a schoolgirl. It was my way of saving face, keeping up appearances, and avoiding embarrassment.

The Heart of the Matter

The truth of it was, if people had been able to see past the secrets and into my heart, they would have seen that it wasn't bad! Yes, I had begun secret-keeping, but the motivation of my heart was to protect others—from worry, from disappointment, from stress, from getting into trouble!

It's often a loving thing to do. Aren't we taught to bear one another's burdens? The question is asked in Scripture, "Am I my brother's keeper?" Often the answer is *yes*. Yes, we are called to love, yes, we are encouraged to bear one another's burdens, yes, we are supposed to keep and care for our brother. But sometimes things that seem good but have misguided intentions can do the opposite of good. Things that were healthy at one time in our lives can become unhealthy at other times.

When I look back at my secret-keeping habits, I know that most of the time I was operating out of love for my parents. In my little-girl thinking, I was lightening their load—giving them one less thing to worry about. *Grown-ups have a lot to think about so why give them another concern?*

But the reality was, it wouldn't have broken them to know the truth. Besides, they were the adults in the scenario, and as adults, the responsibility that I was trying to protect them from was really theirs to carry. If I had gone home that day and told them the truth about my innocent involvement in the lunch order heist, they probably would have just signed the letter and queried my friend choice. It certainly wouldn't have been met with the grave consequences I had imagined, nor would it have added the burdensome weight I was trying to protect them from. In truth, there would have been no threat in bringing it into the open.

While bringing secret things into the light might feel bad at first, it can result in something very good. The Bible teaches us that there is great freedom in living in the light.

> *For you were once darkness, but now you are light in the Lord. Live as children of the light (for the fruit of the light consists in all goodness, righteousness and truth).*
>
> *Ephesians 5:8-9 NIV*

The fruit of bringing things into the light is not condemnation or embarrassment, but goodness, righteousness and truth. The fruit of bringing things into the light is exactly what we were trying to achieve by keeping it all in the darkness!

Isn't it amazing that when we live in the light, we are free from the burden and weight that we have been trying to protect others from all along? But if bringing things into the light equates to freedom, then why are we so worried about saving face? I have realised in my own life that I wasn't just trying to protect others by keeping things hidden; I was also trying to protect *myself*. I was protecting myself from embarrassment, getting into trouble, and feeling that I was not as 'good' as I should have been.

The problem is that saving face usually backfires—as it did for me. The weight of responsibility only got heavier. The burden of the things I kept hidden became only mine to carry, and some of the things I insisted on carrying were too heavy for me alone. Saving face wasn't helping me, it was only weighing me down. Think of King David. He tried to hide his sin. But for David, saving face led to lies, deceit, murder and ultimately loss of the kingdom. It is interesting to me that hiding things somehow leads to the very thing we hoped to avoid!

Bringing Things Into the Light

Our way of doing things is so opposite to God's. When we do it our way, it usually results in making things much worse. We try to be good and only end up bad. Proverbs 28:13 (ESV) says, "Whoever conceals his transgressions will not prosper, but he who confesses and forsakes them will obtain mercy." When I look back, I wonder, *What if I had just said to the police officer, "I'm sorry I was texting, I know that was wrong."?* Worst-case scenario, I would have ended up in the same position but without the shame of lying. The best-case scenario could have been that the police officer was lenient because of my honesty and let me off with a warning. I don't see a downside there, do you?

The same could have been true if I had been honest with my teacher about how I had come to acquire the pizza. What if I had been honest with her about my part in the incident instead of freezing up and saying nothing? What might have happened if I had said, "I am sorry that I ate the pizza, I didn't know that it was stolen from somebody else."? The consequence may have been the same or less—but it certainly wouldn't have been worse. Often, we tell ourselves that the consequences of our honesty are too great to risk revealing the things we keep hidden, and yet we can be harder on ourselves than God is. My experience is that we can spend too much time worrying about things that may not even be an issue. Remember that in God, bringing hidden things to light brings freedom, not restraint.

Think about Peter in the New Testament. Peter was the disciple who denied even knowing Jesus. Three times he said, "I do not know that man." Peter messed up—badly! He hurt his friend, he lied, and then he hid. Peter was so ashamed and broken by his own mistakes that he went back to the trade he knew before he had met Jesus. He discounted himself from all the things Jesus had called him to do. Peter was probably hoping he could just stay hidden from God and all he presumed he had forfeited. But there is no hiding from God—or his grace. After Jesus had risen, he found Peter fishing. And in the gospel of John, we read of this beautiful exchange of the hidden things for the light. Shame for grace. Peter's failings for God's goodness.

And when they had finished eating, Jesus said to Simon Peter, "Simon son of John, do you love me more than these?"

"Yes, Lord," he said, "you know that I love you."

Jesus said, "Feed my lambs."

Again Jesus said, "Simon son of John, do you love me?"

He answered, "Yes, Lord, you know that I love you."

Jesus said, "Take care of my sheep."

The third time he said to him, "Simon son of John, do you love me?"

Peter was hurt because Jesus asked him the third time, "Do you love me?" He said, "Lord, you know all things; you know that I love you."

John 21:15-17 NIV

In doing this, Jesus was allowing Peter to bring into the light what he had covered up. In exchange for the three times Peter had denied Jesus, he was now given the chance to declare his love for him.

What stands out to me in Peter's story is that Peter discounted himself from serving God, and yet God's plan was the opposite! The consequences Peter assigned himself were far worse than those God had allotted to him. How often do we do the same thing? Do we hide, trying to avoid the fallout, when in the meantime, God is simply waiting to exchange our failings for his 'good-ness'?

Who Calls Me Good?

Pleasing people is a habit that many of us form. Often, it's the people in authority over us that we seek approval from the most: a parent, a teacher, a police officer or even a church leader. We strive to please those in a position of authority because we think they have the authority to call us 'good'. I know for certain that ten-year-old Becs thought she was good if those in authority called her good. But *who* ultimately calls us good? I came to realise that it was God who called me good. I am good because *he* is good. It is his goodness and righteousness that ultimately transforms me into his image, making me Christlike. The question is, what does God see when he looks at us?

David asked the same question:

> *Search me, God, and know my heart; test me and know my anxious thoughts. See if there is any offensive way in me and lead me in the way everlasting.*
>
> Psalm 139:23-24 NIV

David presumed that if anyone saw deep into his heart, they would find some bad—that he was ultimately not good. But God saw David's heart; he knew the mistakes that the shepherd king had made. In both 1 Samuel 13 and Acts 13 God still said of him, "I have found a man after my own heart."

David's struggle is an important issue to be aware of. We tend to see the worst in ourselves when God only sees the best.

> *If our hearts condemn us, we know that God is greater than our hearts, and he knows everything.*
>
> 1 John 3:20 NIV

God knows us. He knows every part of us. He *sees* us, and in his sight, we are good. If only I had known that as a ten-year-old girl . . . and as a thirty-six-year-old woman! I had to learn the hard way that the one who calls me good is the One who knows me the best.

The reality is, we are all a little broken and we will continue to make mistakes. The quest for perfection in our own strength is a futile and endless endeavour. It will constantly leave us feeling as though we are not good enough. Be reminded that we don't need authority figures to tell us we are good for it to be true. God, as our heavenly Father, has already declared his goodness over us. If we are going to live burden-free, we must have a clear understanding of how God sees us. At the end of it all, it is his approval that matters most. No matter what we do, or do not do, we are accepted in Christ—and he is good!

Let me say it again: *You are good because God is good.*

III

Keeping Up Appearances

YOU MIGHT NOT BE THE SORT TO LIE TO POLICE OR COVER UP A lunch order theft. But I'm sure all of us have little everyday things we do to keep up appearances. There are so many ways that we put on a mask.

My husband and I had taken our two young sons on a three-month holiday to England to meet my extended family and get to know their cousins, aunties, and uncles. My grandfather had recently been admitted to the hospital, and we were determined to treasure this short time of our wider family being together. That morning, we packed our bags and said goodbye to the family we had been staying with and piled into the rental car to drive to the home of another one of my relatives.

Steve and I settled in for a comfortable two-hour journey, but our conversation unexpectedly devolved into disagreement. Before too long it exploded into an argument. He was mad at me, and I was mad at him. All the while we were drawing closer and closer to our destination. As we drove, I felt more and more urgency to wrap up our heated debate. I could see the house coming into view and our hosts standing outside, excitedly waving at us with big welcoming grins on their faces. Meanwhile, inside the car, Steve and I were each still trying to have the last say as we smiled through gritted teeth. I'm sure the boys in the back seat were gritting their teeth too. We pulled into the drive, got out of the car, and . . .

"Hey! How are you?"

"So good! We're amazing!"

Don't tell me we are the only ones this has happened to! I know you know exactly what I am talking about. You know because every day you get up, get showered and dressed, put on your makeup, do your hair, and right before you leave the house you do what a lot of us do—you throw on your "everything is fine" mask and start your day.

Interestingly, I think that church has always been a place where we go to extra lengths to keep up appearances.

"Hello, how are you?"

"Oh, hello, Sister, I'm blessed. Praise the Lord!"

"God is good."

"All the time."

Sound familiar? Often, when we come to church, we feel pressured to look like we have it all together because it looks like everyone else has it all together. We walk through the doors of the church and when someone asks, "How are you?" we say,

"I'm fine thanks." It is so automatic, isn't it? We don't even have to think much before the words come spilling out of our mouths. We have our church clothes on, our church voices on, our church smiles on, and our church behaviour on, but on the inside we are struggling. We are struggling *and* we are praying that nobody will notice! Our greatest fear is that someone might linger long enough to ask, "But how are you? Really?"

We don't only do this at church. We do it everywhere. A study published by leading UK job board *Totaljobs* showed that thirty-three percent of people hide their real emotions at work, putting on a 'positive face' in front of colleagues.[1] Family gatherings, baby showers, the school gate, the supermarket—these are all places where we hide behind that positive face despite what might be going on just beneath the surface.

The truth for most of us is that we are not trying to cover up terrible, wicked sins. Instead, it's how we are *really* doing that we don't want others to see. We shield those around us from the reality of our feelings, our burdens and our stresses—not letting them in on how we are coping, or not coping. It feels easier sometimes to answer the "How are you?" with, "Yeah, good, everything is great," even when the *real* answer might be more like, "I don't want to talk about it because I am so overwhelmed I might burst into tears". Outwardly you might say, "I'm fine." But inside, you are thinking, *I'm struggling. I feel hurt. I'm exhausted. I'm lonely. It was a battle just to get out of bed this morning.*

---

1 Murray-Nevill J., 2020, January 13. *1 in 3 UK workers hide their true emotions at work.*

Coming to the end of the strict lockdowns we had here in New Zealand during the Covid-19 pandemic, I recall friends and family talking about the relief they felt in being able to get back to normal life and start doing things again. On the other hand, I distinctly remember I wanted the opposite. I didn't want to go back to the outside world. I liked having a genuine excuse not to show up to things. All I wanted to do was keep hiding in lockdown because going back to normal living meant my schedule would become full again. It meant more appointments and more meetings. In all honesty, pastoring churches became harder during the pandemic. With restrictions on gathering, vaccination certificates, masks, and political tensions, there just seemed to be more problems for me to navigate. I remember pouring my internal battle out to God in my prayer journal:

> *"Lord, I am struggling in this current season. I am struggling to feel passion and motivation for anything other than staying in bed. I am so tired all the time. Getting up every morning is a battle and then when I get up I don't want to do anything other than the tasks where I don't have to think. I am struggling to step back into the world we live in. I want to hide. I want to stay in bed. I want to stay hidden from where people can get to me."*

This reflected a lot of my conversations with the Lord at that time in my life. I was over having to hold it all together. I was tired of it all. I wanted to stay hidden. I wanted to tuck myself away where no one could reach me.

Hiding ourselves away isn't just a response to overwhelm that shows in our feelings. This habit of keeping up appearances can also be an extension of our desire to protect others. I found myself keeping my struggles to myself because I simply did not want to add my burden onto someone else. The last thing I wanted was for people to feel sorry for me or, worse, for them to feel the need to fix my issues. I got used to *not* asking for help, *not* sharing the load, *not* letting people in. It is especially hard as a pastor to walk away knowing you have been real but wondering if you have lost credibility in the eyes of those you shared with. *Did I say too much? Was I too honest? Should I have just said nothing?*

Would you believe that even as I wrote this book, I began to second guess whether I should include some of the stories from my more difficult times? I doubted whether it was the right thing for me to be so vulnerable. I questioned whether I wanted to pull off the mask and let people in. The truth is—this is uncomfortable. I don't like the thought of people knowing about those parts of me. I don't want people to feel sorry for me or pity me.

Most of the time we don't want or need the problem fixed, we just need to feel seen, heard and validated. It's the safety of the right kind of environment for taking off the mask that encourages us to share in a real way. One where we are not offered pity, solutions, and judgement. It has taken me years to get my lovely husband to understand that most of the time my tears and meltdowns do not require him to solve my problem, but to simply listen to me and reassure me that I am okay. The last thing I need is for him to jump to my rescue by cancelling my schedule or setting me up on a coffee catch-up with a friend for support. His heart was always in the right place, but I didn't want yet *another* thing to do, I just wanted a big cry and a shameless vent!

We can all play a role in this. Each of us can create that safe space for another. How can we help each other take off the mask?

1. Acknowledgement

Often, a person who places high value on qualities such as responsibility and conscientiousness feels a great desire to be acknowledged. I know that is certainly true for me. I don't need much in this world, but to have my hard work, abilities and contribution recognised can go a long way in making me feel seen, heard and valued.

The same is true whether I am thriving or just surviving. Often when I have felt overwhelmed to the point of meltdown, it isn't a change in schedule or a transfer of responsibility that has helped me to overcome my struggle; it has been a genuine comment like, "Gosh, that sounds really hard," which has helped. To hear words like that made me feel like a burden came off, even if the physical or practical weight is still on. The acknowledgement says, "I see you. I see your work. I see your sacrifice and it is appreciated." *Being seen* by someone goes a long way towards sharing the load.

2. Solidarity

Think about a time you felt nervous or had feelings of fear when you thought you were alone in a situation. Perhaps as a child, you didn't like being alone in the dark. Or maybe as you were growing up you experienced the worry of trying something new all on your own. Now imagine the relief you felt when someone you trusted appeared and reassured you. You were now not alone. Not only were you not alone, you were in the company of someone who had once been in your same situation and come through. It brings great comfort, doesn't it?

The enemy, also known as 'the father of lies', will attempt to convince us that we are alone in our struggle. He uses shame to keep us hiding ourselves and therefore isolated. We feel shame because when we look around us, we think that everyone else has it together and that we are the only ones who can't seem to do what we know we need to.

But can I let you in on a secret? We are all a little messed up. We all have brokenness. We all struggle under the weight of something at one time or another. I have discovered that often all we need is to realise we are not in our struggle alone. It is amazing how much comfort and security the words 'me too' can give a person! They have a way of making you feel normal. You are no longer alone, no longer the only one. Somehow the pressure comes off.

There's an age-old saying that goes, "A problem shared is a problem halved". I genuinely believe there is a lot of truth to that. All of a sudden, the weight we were carrying alone becomes a weight we now carry together. When someone shows solidarity with our circumstances, we realise that our issue is not isolated, and it is not impossible to get through. We can look to the testimony of others to reassure us of our survival.

3. Encouragement

One of the greatest gifts we can give one another is the gift of encouragement. My husband often says, "Encouragement is the very act of putting courage into one another." When I am in a place of feeling that I cannot take one more step, I need someone to come along and remind me that I can. We can do this for one another. I know that when I am feeling crushed under the pressure of responsibility, my greatest need in that moment is not for someone to come along and take away the things I am carrying. That response often makes me feel like I have failed and what I hear in that moment is, "You can't do this, let me do it for you."

But if someone were to simply say to me, "Wow, that's hard. But you can do hard things. You have got this. You are doing so much better than you think you are," then suddenly I am reassured of my ability. I am filled with the courage to hold on and not give up, and I am strengthened by someone else's belief that I can do it. Rather than handing over the things I am accountable for and feeling like a failure because of it, I feel I can keep going and finish what I started, which gives me a sense of achievement.

It is likely that in most circumstances, we don't need a quick fix, we just need to know that we are seen and supported, that someone believes in us. And perhaps in that kind of environment, we could come to a place where it's okay to take off the mask. It's okay to stop hiding. It's okay to ask for help. It's okay to 'not be able to'. It's okay to reach a limit in our capacity. I am not sure about you but that is already bringing freedom to my soul.

IV

Hiding Things

IT'S UNDERSTANDABLE TO FEEL RELUCTANT TO SHARE OUR LIVES with others, but why do we find it so hard to be vulnerable with God? After all, he knows us inside out anyway. He already knows the things we are trying to keep from him. Us hiding things from God is a bit like you or I playing hide and seek with a toddler. God can already see every part of us despite our best attempts to squeeze behind the couch! Even though we may be Christians who have known his grace and freedom in other areas of our lives, we still have so many things that we don't want to bring before him.

When it came time for me to pack boxes for moving house, I called on a friend to help. She was both a minimalist and ruthless when it came to decluttering spaces—she was perfect for the job. We quickly got stuck into packing up my kitchen, and it wasn't long before we began discovering all the things I had forgotten even existed. As my friend reached into the back of the high-up cupboards, we laughed at the strange assortment of belongings she found—all the things I had tucked away in a safe place out of reach, out of sight, and apparently, completely out of mind.

They were forgotten and forever lost to the dark and dusty space above the fridge.

We all have a place like that in our home, a top shelf or high-up cupboard most likely in the kitchen—the place where you hide all the things you don't want your children to know you have. And don't try and tell me you don't also have a stash of chocolate somewhere that you binge on when your kids aren't looking! It's the place you put the things you don't want anyone else to see or discover. A place for the things you no longer need but can't quite bring yourself to let go of. All of it goes on that top shelf, just out of reach. As I write these words, I am thinking about the packet of mini-chocolate bars I have hidden in the cupboard above the microwave.

But it isn't just in our kitchens or our homes that we have high places where we put all the things we want to keep just out of reach. For most of us, we have those places in our lives too—made up of a combination of things we want to keep out of reach and things we want to keep hidden. We have high places and hidden spaces.

As I reflected on the hidden things in my kitchen, I became aware that the secrecy habit I had developed not only expressed itself in my keeping things from others but also extended to keeping things from God. I was faced with the question: Do I have 'high places' like the high cupboards in my kitchen, where I am putting all the things that I don't want God to have access to? Do I have hidden spaces in my life that I am keeping off -limits from God?

Not only do we try to cover our sins and the shameful areas of our lives, but there are also the many deeper issues of our hearts that we try to keep hidden from God. Things like our long-awaited hopes and dreams, disappointments and discouragement, our sense of inadequacy or shortcoming, even our long-held religious traditions.

The Traditions We Hold Tightly

I love traditions. I love them because they are memorable. I want my children to grow up and pass them on to their children. I want them to tell their kids and grandkids about all the ways we celebrated and acknowledged the special moments in their lives. I think I also like them because I like routine. When it's routine, it's predictable. I can count on it, so I want to hold tightly to it. I like the way I do it; I like the way it's always been done.

I think it's safe to say that there are certain church traditions we like to hold tightly to. We come to the same church service, we sit in the same seat, we sing our favourite songs, and we laugh at our favourite preacher's jokes. But Lord help us all if they try to change something without our vote! We like it the way we like it, and we don't want it to change!

Not all tradition is bad, but tradition will trip us up if it causes us to become stuck in our ways and prevents us from hearing and obeying the leading of the Lord. If there is anything in our life that is not subject to change—even by God—then it has moved from being a tradition to becoming an idol. I had to ask myself if I had become stuck in any immovable traditions. Did the Lord want me to submit to him? It's probably obvious that anyone who likes everything under control, predictable, and in a routine, would have 'high places' like this, right?

I want to ask you: What traditions have you put in high places that God might be asking you to lay down? What about that family tradition you've held onto for generations? What about the habits you don't want to let go of? What about the comforts of life you really enjoy?

The Prayers We Haven't Seen Answered Yet

It's the things that mean the most to us that are hardest to let go of: the hopes and dreams we have been holding onto; the yearnings tucked deep down in our hearts, safe from disappointment, safe from regret, and safe from the pain of delayed answers.

I am reminded of a story in 2 Kings 4, about a woman who had a prayer on her heart that she couldn't voice out loud. She was holding a hope to herself so tightly that she couldn't bear to part with it. She desperately wanted a child but had never been able to conceive. We are told that she would show hospitality to the prophet Elisha every time he was in town. She made sure he had a place to stay, eat, and rest awhile. Elisha was so taken with the welcome from this woman that he wanted to do something to thank her for her kindness. His helper Gehazi mentioned to Elisha that she had no son. Elisha asked that she be brought to him. She came, and as she stood in the doorway, he said to her, "About this time next year you will hold a son in your arms."

"No, my lord," she replied, "man of God, do not lie to your servant" (v. 15).

What was she saying? She was saying, please don't get my hopes up! It sounds to me that she had prayed many times and for many years, but delays and seeming denials had caused her to climb up to the top shelf and pop that prayer safely up there where her hopes couldn't be dashed anymore.

Ever had a prayer like that? Something you have been believing for and yet you have seen disappointment at so many turns you have decided that prayer is too painful for even God to hear? Have you ever decided to take something off your prayer list and put it on a high shelf because you don't want to get your hopes up again? You have clung to it in the secret places in your own heart, refusing to open it up to God to let him in.

In our story, the woman receives the answer to her prayer, and a son born one year later. But that's not the end of it—the child grew, and one day while out in the fields, he complained of a sore head and died in his mother's arms soon after. That hardly seems fair, does it? She finally gets the child she had longed for and he dies before he reaches adolescence!

What does she do? She goes to find Elisha. This time, instead of keeping her desperate prayer to herself, she takes the dying promise and goes straight to the One who had promised her a son in the first place. The story goes on to tell us that when Elisha arrives and prays for the boy, he is raised back to life.

Here is my gentle encouragement to you: Perhaps it's time to take those unanswered prayers, hopes and dreams out of hiding, and surrender them to God again. Maybe it's time to take the longed-for promise to the One who promised it in the first place. Know this: of all the things we can do with our hopes and dreams, offering them to the Giver of those hopes and dreams is by far the safest.

All the Little Things

Have you found that it's the little things that stay hidden for the longest? That little thing we've become so familiar with that we begin to justify holding onto it. We convince ourselves that it isn't so bad, it's just little after all. Things like unforgiveness, pride, gossip, stubbornness, jealousy, or even our sense of inadequacy and shortcomings.

It is so easy for us to become accustomed to and even comfortable with these things in our lives that, rather than submitting them to God and risk facing up to them—because let's be honest that's not fun—we put them in a box, tuck them way up into a high place and hope they will be forgotten. We leave them unsubmitted and un-surrendered. The truth is that deep down we know that if we reveal them, we must deal with them.

Imagine unpacking boxes after moving to a new house when you have not put the time or effort into going through the junk in advance and getting rid of all the things you don't want to drag along with you into the next house. It's a huge task. Every time you open a box you've got to deal with its contents. The reality is, it's hard work to confront our issues and it can feel completely overwhelming . . . which is why I am sure I am not the only one with unopened boxes sitting in my garage that have been transported from house to house and never once unpacked.

Why Do We Keep Things From God?

Why do we do this? Why do we insist on keeping things so well hidden that it almost feels impossible to bring them into the light? I wonder if it's because we ultimately want God to see us as 'good'. Perhaps we think that if we bring those things to God, his first response will be judgment and condemnation rather than mercy and grace. This would be especially true if being 'good' was a primary and core value in our little world—it certainly was for me.

Maybe the real reason we don't bring everything to God is that our view of God hasn't grown and matured as we have grown and matured. We still view God much as we did when we were children. In the eyes and mind of a child, he is a big, strong God. Perhaps we believed that he lived up in the sky somewhere watching down over us, looking to see how good we were, because if we were good little girls and boys we would get good things—right? But then, we grow up and begin adulting. As we get older, we experience life's ups and downs. We are confronted with the realities of a broken world. We are met with struggle, loss, pain and disappointment. If our view of God doesn't grow and mature as we do, then we will struggle to reconcile and relate our childhood God with our adult realities.

We can still see him as the great big God who sits in heaven looking down over us. All those same feelings and responses we had as a child—of doing something wrong, getting into trouble, and trying to be good—are carried over into adulthood. If we don't adapt and grow in our relationship with God, we will, without realising it, continue to relate to him as a child. Perhaps this is why in 1 Corinthians 13 (CSB), we read:

> *"When I was a child, I spoke like a child, I thought like a child, I reasoned like a child. When I became a man, I put aside childish things."*

In putting childish things aside, we can grow in our view of God and of how we relate to him. We are no longer immature children trying to please a scary or far-off God. We are sons and daughters growing in grace on a journey to become more like Christ.

When we bring things into the light before God, we find that he is more gracious, more loving and much more ready than we realise to do a transforming work in us. What if his response is more like the response we'd receive from a loving parent than the schoolteacher we were afraid of? What if, in bringing things to God, we are met with a reassurance of his love, and a reminder of our place of belonging in his family? What if bringing things into the light wasn't such a burden after all?

It reminds me of the scene in the film *Beauty and the Beast,* when the Beast is showing Belle around her new 'home'. He invites her to see many rooms and many spaces . . . until they get to the west wing. The moment Belle glances toward it curiously, the Beast shouts, "You must never go there!" and quickly hides from view whatever might be behind those doors. As the story unfolds, the Beast eventually allows Belle into the room he had wanted to keep hidden. In doing so, he allows Belle to see more of who he is and therefore understand him at a deeper level. The beautiful part about their story is that what Belle learnt about the Beast did not drive her away from him—it made her love him more.

What have you been reluctant to bring to God? Could it be that bringing these things to God may be the catalyst for the deeper intimacy we crave with him? I want to remind you that your mistakes and mess-ups do not shock or surprise God. He is not thrown by the stuff you bring to him—it pleases him to see the very deepest parts of you without restraint or reserve. If you will give him the opportunity, you can be reassured that you haven't blown it. He still has a purpose for your life and he can still use you. We write ourselves off too easily, when in fact, God hasn't finished with us yet. He is the God of redemption and re-writes. We can trust him to kindly and graciously take us by the hand and lead us in the deep work of going through our lives box by box and dealing with our 'stuff' so that we can walk unburdened into our future, secure in the knowledge that we are his—seen, known, and *still* loved.

V

The Problem with Trying to Do It All

I T HAD BEEN A FEW MONTHS SINCE MY PANIC ATTACK IN OUR bedroom, and during my morning quiet time I had been reflecting on the conversation from my counselling session the previous day. My counsellor was helping me work through why I felt so much anxiety every time someone got in touch to ask for a meeting. It wasn't that I was worried the meeting would be about something negative or that I wouldn't know how to respond. It was something more. During our session, it became clear, in my mind at least, that whenever someone came to me with a problem, I made myself responsible to fix it. There was this dread that someone might need something from me that I simply couldn't give. I wasn't worried about doing more work. It was the emotional weight of feeling like whatever landed on me was mine to ultimately solve.

When my husband, Steve, runs leadership training with our staff, he often uses the expression, "Stop adopting monkeys."

He suggests that one of the mistakes we make as leaders is when someone comes to us with a problem—or as he puts it, a 'monkey'—we allow that monkey to somehow end up on our back. The person might have left our office or the conversation but they have deposited their monkey with us. Steve says, "Not your circus, not your monkey." You know what? I had been walking around with a whole bunch of adopted monkeys on my back!

That morning, in my time with God, it was as if a light bulb came on in my mind. I came running out of our bedroom into the main living area shouting, "Steve, I literally do this *with everything!*" It was as though the blindfold had been removed, and I suddenly had become aware of a behaviour that I had exhibited my whole life but was completely unaware of. I had spent the past thirty-six years telling myself that I was responsible for everything. And when I say everything, I mean everything. Every outcome. Every problem. Every task. Even every form that needed filling out!

In my head, everything was my job and my responsibility. I did it in my home with our household responsibilities: the washing, the cleaning, the cooking, our finances. I did it with our children: the school lunches, the drop-offs and pickups, the feeding, changing, and bathing. I did it in my leadership: taking charge of things, problem-solving for others and jumping in when someone needed something. I did it in personal relationships: peacekeeping, smoothing things over, making sure everything was okay. (This revelation was not as much of a surprise to my husband as it was to me!)

If false responsibility is defined as feeling responsible for things that, objectively, you aren't responsible for and shouldn't feel responsible for, then I was the poster girl for false responsibility.

The Pitfalls of "Leave It with Me"

By this point in my life, my default response had become, "Leave it with me". What's so wrong with that? I mean, I was being helpful. Supportive and loving toward those around me. I was making myself available. I could be relied on, I could take care of things. But the 'leave-it-with-me' mindset has some serious pitfalls.

1. It's a Trap

The problem with saying "leave-it-with-me" was that, funnily enough, I ended up being left with it. All of it. And it wasn't because others dumped it on me and I was an unwilling participant, it was because I had taken it from them. One problem led to another, and before I knew it, I was trapped in a cycle that I couldn't 'to-do-list' my way out of.

This high sense of responsibility has a way of making us feel imprisoned by our bad habits. It might begin with the feeling that we are being helpful. After all we are doing a good thing. But I learnt in my journey that the more false responsibility we take on, the more we are chaining ourselves to the mindset—we're just digging ourselves a deeper hole. We become trapped because the more we do it the more we are now left carrying, and the more we are carrying, the more mess we make when we drop it. This creates a mounting pressure to hold it all together and not let anything fall. At least that's how I felt.

I remember the day my counsellor asked me, "What would it feel like to put down one of those things you're carrying?" Before I could even think, the words came out of my mouth, "It would feel scary". The thought was terrifying because 'carrying it' was the only way I knew to keep everything tidy in my little world.

In *Psychology Today*, researcher and educator Tania Luna describes the cycle we become enslaved in:

> ". . . worst of all, hyper-responsibility is self-reinforcing. The obsession (guilt), leads to the compulsion (taking responsibility), which alleviates the guilt, which in turn reinforces the belief that taking responsibility makes those bad feelings go away. In a sense, taking responsibility becomes an addicting escape from persistent feelings of guilt. What's more, responsible people also tend to be rewarded by others for being considerate or 'saving the day'."[2]

Her words made so much sense to me. They reminded me of some lines from the book of Habakkuk. There, the prophet is complaining to God about injustices against his people. We read this back-and-forth conversation between Habakkuk and God. Habakkuk complains and God responds. In God's first response to Habakkuk, he speaks about the Babylonians:

---

2 Luna, T. "Are You Guilt-Prone or Hyper-Responsible?" *Psychology Today*, February 3, 2022.

They sweep past like the wind and are gone. But they are
deeply guilty, for their own strength is their god.

Habakkuk 1:11

That last phrase in his response stuck with me: ". . . for their own strength is their god." Perhaps this is the problem that all capable people have. We make our own strength into an idol of sorts. Our ability to do things well and to hold it all together, our capacity to wear multiple hats and pull it off with what looks like little effort—we rely on it, we put our trust in it, placing it above everything else in our lives. Above our families, above our marriages, above our self-care and well-being. We might even go so far as to protect our reputation for being capable. When others ask, "Are you sure you're not doing too much?" we get spikey and defensive. We want others to see that we actually *can* do it all, and to glorify us for it. I know I am guilty of that! The problem is that we can soon end up falling into the hole we've inadvertently dug.

2. It Prevents Self-Care

Having a high sense of responsibility, or hyper-responsibility as Tania Luna puts it, doesn't allow us to easily take rest or practise self-care. I remember many occasions when, out of sheer exhaustion, I would melt down to my husband because I was overloaded. He would suggest that I cancel a meeting or not attend a pre-existing appointment to allow myself time to rest. Every time he suggested it, I struggled to follow through. We would go back and forth over the decision. In the end, I wouldn't cancel or pull out on the commitments. I just couldn't bring myself to do it—my hyper-responsibility wouldn't let me. *Responsible people keep their word, they can be relied on. If they cancel, then what good is that?* I thought. I would rather have turned up at the expense of my wellbeing and sanity than disappoint someone by changing plans.

It took me years to realise that this aspect of my personality that I believed was so 'good' was preventing me from being 'good' physically, mentally, and emotionally. It was constantly hindering me from prioritising the self-care I needed to function well for those who genuinely needed me.

The practice of self-care was something Jesus did—and taught his disciples to do. In Mark 6, Jesus commissions his disciples to go out and heal the sick and cast out demons. They went out in pairs preaching and ministering. After some time, they came back to Jesus and told him all of the many things that had happened. Upon hearing about their experiences, Jesus says to them, "Come away by yourselves to a remote place and rest for a while." The rest of the verse gives us the context:

> *For many people were coming and going, and they did not even have time to eat.*
>
> *Mark 6:31* CSB

It seems to me that while healing the sick and leading people to repentance was of utmost importance, Jesus knew that personal and physical restoration was equally necessary and vital to what he was teaching his disciples. If we are to avoid the pitfalls of trying to do it all, we need to learn to think differently about the guilt of disappointing others, and prioritise our self-care.

3. It's a Fast-track to Resentment

The person in the Bible that I relate to the most is Martha. Oh, Martha, I get you!

We read her story in Luke 10. Jesus and his disciples were visiting the home of Martha and her sister Mary. Both sisters welcomed Jesus and his friends into their home, but Martha quickly became distracted with all of the preparations for the big dinner she had planned. In the meantime, her sister Mary simply sat at Jesus' feet listening to his teachings. Soon, however, Martha became annoyed. Coming to Jesus, she said,

> *"Lord, doesn't it seem unfair to you that my sister just sits here while I do all the work? Tell her to come and help me."*
> *Luke 10:40*

It would seem that Martha had worked herself into a place of frustration and resentment. She complains to Jesus that Mary is not helping her with any of the work and instead is leaving her to carry it all on her own.

Is it just me or is anyone else feeling like this story is getting a bit close to the nerve? I know I have felt all the things Martha was feeling: overworked, under-appreciated, frustrated, disappointed, under-valued and let down.

When we hold such high expectations of ourselves, we often transfer that same level of expectation onto others. And when *they* don't meet the expectations they didn't even know they were falling short of, *we* feel disappointed. When we have such a high sense of responsibility, we struggle to understand why others don't live their lives with the same sense of duty and obligation—in our humble opinion, of course.

It means we can easily feel let down and disappointed by others who don't measure up to our high expectations. The feeling of disappointment quickly leads to resentment. Resentment for all the things we are doing that others aren't. Resentment about all the ways others have unknowingly let us down. Resentment because we are doing all the work and no one even notices.

Like Martha, all of a sudden, things that once brought us joy now bring bitterness. People we found a blessing in serving now become a burden. A role we used to love now feels like a chore. How sad it is that Martha missed the gift of communing with Jesus. *Jesus*, the in-the-flesh-Jesus, was in her home, and yet she allowed resentment to rob her of the joy of his presence. Resentment always has a way of stealing our enjoyment, but if we can learn to deal with it, we will also find that we rediscover our joy in both the big and the small things.

The truth is, living 'irresponsibly' involves recognising we cannot do it all; in fact, there are many pitfalls if we try. Discovering a lighter way to live will help us to avoid those pitfalls and live freely in the calling that God has for us.

Please hear me: responsibility is not a bad thing. It can be a very good thing—it got me where I am today. It has taught me to be hardworking and dependable. It tells of my stewardship and faithfulness to see things through and get the job done. But I had to realise that the mindset of hyper-responsibility was no longer serving me. It was leaving me feeling trapped in a cycle of compulsion and guilt. I lacked the boundaries I needed to stay healthy, and I could tell that bitterness and resentment were beginning to take root in my heart. I needed to find a way out of the hole I was digging. I needed to rediscover the joy that my life warranted. I wanted to stop begrudging what God had called me to do and start enjoying my wonderful life again.

VI

Confusion and Calling

HAVE YOU EVER TRIED PACKING FOR A TRIP ONLY TO FIND YOURSELF in a predicament? You've picked out what you'd like to take. The suitcase is open, and you have a pile of folded clothing on the bed. Now you've got to figure out what goes in and what stays because whatever you pack now, you have to carry later. There's no way you can take it all with you—that does not stop me from trying though.

Before my husband took over the role of Senior Pastor, we went away on an eleven-week sabbatical. We were heading to England for a winter Christmas, followed by a cruise through the Caribbean on our way home. You can imagine my dilemma at having to pack for a freezing winter *and* a tropical summer without exceeding my weight limit! I have always been an over-packer and inevitably find myself regretting it later when I am wheeling two suitcases, two hand luggage bags and a neck pillow across a busy airport.

The same is true when we are transitioning into any new season of life. If we are going to be true to our calling yet not be overwhelmed with responsibilities, we need to ask ourselves: *What is coming with me? What should I leave behind? What is essential? What is adding weight that might be too much for me to carry?* I know all too well the regret of picking up responsibility for something and then, when reality hits, asking myself, *Why on earth did I say yes to this?* Some things just aren't meant to come with us into the next season.

If the Lord is asking us to lean into something new then perhaps it's time to leave something else behind. You can't take everything with you, can you? Practically, it's just not possible. We know that about the stuff in our suitcase, but it seems to be hard for us to grasp when it comes to responsibilities.

God is always wanting to grow us and entrust us with more, but he also wants us to travel light. He desires that in each new season, we have enough space in our life to enjoy all that the season offers. He wants us to be available for all he's calling us into. There is so much blessing and enlargement with each new season—but it often doesn't feel that way.

I remember reading Jesus' words:

> *"From everyone who has been given much, much will be required; and from the one who has been entrusted with much, even more will be expected."*
> Luke 12:48 CSB

As a 'responsibile workaholic', this verse felt like a heavy burden. I could feel the weight of taking on new responsibilities when there were already so many I couldn't *not* be responsible for.

Much was already required of me. With my husband stepping into his new role, would even more be expected? What did that mean for me in my already overwhelmed state? Was it okay for me to put down some of the things that felt too much for me to bear? I knew this was the greater calling on my life, but what about the things that I was already responsible for, and how could I tell the difference?

Confusion comes when we cannot differentiate between our actual responsibilities and the responsibilities that come with each new season. There are many responsibilities in life that we can't just avoid, right? I tell my kids that all the time when I say, "Boys, life is full of doing things we don't want to do but that's just life." I can't just stop adulting because God is leading me into a new thing or because I'm approaching midlife and dramatically working through my childhood trauma! Where do we draw the line between carrying too much and carrying what is our genuine responsibility?

We can look at three different aspects to help us define that line: calling, capacity and credit.

Understanding Our Calling

Knowing your God-given assignment in each season is important when it comes to determining levels of responsibility. Understanding your assignment will help you with your yes and your no. It will also help you to feel confident that you are being faithful to what you have been entrusted with. There are a lot of things that I could do as a pastor. I could travel, preaching in different churches. I could host conferences or appear on podcasts. But in this season, it helps me to remember that I am called to lead my local church. Right now, I know God is asking me to be faithful in serving the congregation he has placed us in. This helps me when I am conflicted about where I should spend my time. It helps me when someone asks me to do something outside of that assignment. That's not to say that I can't do other things, or that I won't at some point, but it does mean that I don't have to feel the weight of all those extra things because I know what God is asking of me in this season. My biggest responsibility is to be obedient and faithful to what the Lord has entrusted me with now.

Knowing Our Capacity

When I am packing that suitcase for my holiday, at some point I must acknowledge that it is only so big. There will come a time when I cannot physically fit anything else into that bag—it will have reached its capacity. The struggle for the hyper-responsible person is the admission that their bag is full. We tend to think: No worries, I can fill another suitcase. Run out of hands? Not a problem, that's what backpacks are for. Understanding capacity is important, especially when we are stepping into a new season, because it isn't just about learning *what* to carry, we also have to learn *how much* we can carry.

That's not to say that our capacity can't change. Capacity often changes between seasons. There have been times when my capacity has felt bigger and times when my capacity has felt smaller. There have also been times when God has been growing my capacity so that I can carry more. It is important to recognise when our capacity is reaching its limit—when the suitcase is getting full. Having the self-awareness to read our cues is essential. I know that when I am coming close to my maximum capacity I tend to become grumpy and feel more tired than usual. If we don't want to end up feeling anxious and overwhelmed, we must begin to adjust some things in our lives and be willing to lighten the load.

Building Up Credit

It's helpful to think of staying within our calling and our gifting as 'building up credit'. It's like having money in the bank. Over time, as we invest carefully in our assignments, our 'credit' grows. And over time, this enables us to make withdrawals without feeling like we are in deficit. We have something to draw from when God calls us to give out more in a certain area. On the other hand, if we try to engage often in things that we are not called to or gifted in, then it feels like we are drawing from an empty account—and we end up in overdraft! I'm not gifted heavily in a pastoral care capacity. In my role as a pastor I regularly meet one-on-one with people to pray for them and offer support, but if I try to do that with each person on an ongoing basis, I quickly run out of credit and am left feeling drained. In seasons when I have had to make lots of pastoral care withdrawals, I have often been left thinking, *What they're asking me for, I don't have.*

Having an awareness of where your credit stores lie is especially important when seasons change. This knowledge will help you as you work out what responsibilities will be coming with you into the new season. Is there something you do that fills your cup, rather than leaving you feeling 'poured out'?

Navigating a Change in Seasons

One of the most helpful realisations for me was the understanding that responsibilities change as seasons change. Discerning that change is key.

I ran an annual women's conference for our movement for twelve years. By then, it had grown in size and we had established it in three different cities over two consecutive weekends. I loved the conference, but there came a point when there was no longer ease to it and the fit became uncomfortable. I lost the drive I once had and I no longer had a vision for it. I knew because of my gifting, knowledge and history that I could have held onto the leadership of that conference, but it would have left me in deficit. I could sense that the grace for me to be the leader had gone. Even trying to envision the next year left me feeling depleted. It was time for me to hand it on.

Sometimes the season to carry something changes and it is no longer right for us to continue with it. God will grace us, equipping us by the power of his Holy Spirit to do what we need to do for just the right time. I have watched friends journey through immense loss and yet still minister profoundly, as though God was supernaturally gifting them with the grace they needed. I have also watched friends continue to struggle and strive to hold onto a season that they are no longer graced to carry. They become tired, frustrated and unable to discern the change required.

Other times, God will actually bring us new responsibilities in order to grow our capacity and show us that we can carry more than we thought we could. Instead of overwhelming us, those new responsibilities take us to new levels of stewardship.

We see this in the Bible time and time again. In Judges 6 we read the story of Gideon threshing wheat in a winepress. Why is he threshing wheat in a winepress, not on the threshing floor? It is because he is fearful and overwhelmed. He is hiding from the enemy, the Midianite tribe. It is notable that when the angel of God visits Gideon in his moment of overwhelm, he doesn't downsize the calling on this man's life. Instead, he affirms it. The angel of the Lord did not instruct Gideon to put his calling down. He instructed him in such a way that it prepared him for what God wanted to do next. He strengthened and expanded his capacity.

I have often felt like Gideon—overwhelmed, fearful, and desperate to hide. If no one can find me, then no one can expect anything from me! There are many times when I have felt maxed out and yet God continues to give me more than I think I can bear. So what happens when what I have been asked to steward has come from God but it's all too much? This passage from 1 Corinthians comes to mind:

> *No temptation has come upon you except what is common to humanity. But God is faithful; he will not allow you to be tempted beyond what you are able, but with the temptation he will also provide the way out so that you may be able to bear it.*
>
> *1 Corinthians 10:13 CSB*

We can assume that this verse is speaking about the temptation to sin, however, it also tells me something about God's nature. If he is faithful to provide a way out from the temptation of sin, then I know he is also faithful to provide a way out as I navigate the challenges of a changing season.

I am sure I am not the only one who faces the temptation to overload myself and take into a new season the responsibilities that he's asked me to leave behind. Many times in my life I have found myself tripping over that very temptation, and in my many years in ministry, I have seen others do the same. We fail to recognise the change that comes with each new season. This is something we will face time and time again as we mature and grow through life. Responsibilities as a single person look different to those of a married person. Day-to-day life with children looks different to the life you lived before kids. Toddlers are different to school-aged kids and then change comes again as they become teenagers. Sickness can throw life's usual rhythms out. If we do not recognise the changes that must come with each new season, we will end up struggling under the weight of unmet expectations and the feelings of failure and guilt that we don't measure up.

When I first felt the Lord leading me to write this book, I knew it would take a lot of time and energy to get all the content out and onto the page. I also knew that if I was going to be obedient and faithful with what I knew God was calling me to, then I needed to be deliberate about making some changes to my daily rhythms and schedule. I had to take my overflowing suitcase and do some rearranging and repacking. Certain things that I had been carrying had to be put down for that season. Things like rostering myself off the preaching schedule or refraining from binge-watching Netflix shows. These changes meant that I wasn't just piling more into my already full suitcase, they meant that I could freely enter into the season God was calling me to because I had made room to do so.

Sometimes letting things go or putting something down can feel irresponsible. But I have found that God in his faithfulness opens a way for us to put down responsibility without leaving others in the lurch. Our God is not irresponsible, and he cares more about the details than we do. In providing a way out, I have faith that God always opens up the way—often through other people or unexpected provision.

Is God wanting to give you more grace for the season you are in, or is he providing a way out? We can trust him to step in and shoulder the responsibility ensuring his purposes still flourish. And in doing so God allows us to live 'ir-responsibly'. Imagine that! It sounds liberating, doesn't it?

VII

Running Commentary

M Y YOUNGEST SON IS TWELVE YEARS OLD AND AN ADORABLE chatterbox. He talks non-stop unless he's sleeping— although he has also been known to sleep talk! Even when no one else is in the room, he is still going, offering a running commentary about what he is doing, what others are doing, what he is going to do, and what he is imagining he will do. He commentates while we are driving, while we are eating, while we are watching television, or playing on the PlayStation. I have even heard his commentary coming from the bathroom!

Not too dissimilar from the constant chattering I hear from my son is *my* constant internal narrative. While my little boy's commentary is charming and cute, my inner narrative hasn't always been so helpful. In fact, for many years it was damaging and ugly.

Our internal narratives can originate from our hearts and emotions, from someone else's comment to us, or they can simply be old proverbial sayings that became part of us while we are growing up. My nan had plenty of these. "Horseplay always ends in tears," she'd say. I heard Nan, my aunties, and my parents say it so often that I now catch myself shouting it to my children when I hear them slamming one another into the coffee table mid-wrestle.

There are so many sayings like this though, aren't there? Sayings like: 'Better late than never', 'A job worth doing is worth doing well', or 'Don't cry over spilt milk'. While some sayings might incorporate a little wisdom, they can often lead us to develop ingrained beliefs about our world that may not always be helpful . . . or even true.

Ultimately, all untruths originate from our spiritual enemy, Satan, who is identified as 'the father of lies' (John 8:44). The reality is that these destructive narratives can run on repeat in our minds for years—even generations—without our knowledge or awareness of how much they are directing our actions, interactions, and responses. This was certainly true for me.

Two Lies

After the revelation of my tendency toward hyper-responsibility, I spent some time undoing the commentary that I had on repeat. While unpacking the narratives, I discovered that there were two lies that I had unknowingly been living by for years.

Lie #1: If I don't do it, no one else will

This was a big one for me. And the moment I said it out loud for the first time I began to see it in my response to everything.

"If I don't do it no one else will." It was the narrative that had shaped how I approached my entire life—in our home, with my children, and in my workplace. It was how I parented, how I led people in ministry, and how I approached chores at home. Everything.

If I don't do it no one else will. This implies that everything depends on us. It means if we don't act or respond then everything stagnates, forward motion stops, and progress and production stall. That's a lot of pressure for one person to bear. Over time we become the self-appointed, problem-solving hero and rescuer to everyone around us.

I can remember on multiple occasions becoming frustrated when I felt like I was the only one doing the housework. I would mutter things to myself like, "Well I guess it's me on the dishes again. God only knows, if I don't do it, it won't get done." But this is one of those lies that becomes like a self-fulfilling prophecy—we convince ourselves that others won't do it, so we jump in and do it without even giving them a chance to prove us wrong. Over time people begin to depend on us to continue doing those things because that's what we have always done. And let's be honest, they often don't do it to our standards anyway. We end up working ourselves into a position where everyone is so dependent on us that they can't possibly cope without us doing what we have always insisted we do. After all, why would they think to do it when we always do? And so the cycle continues, the narrative repeats and it all confirms the lie we told ourselves to begin with: *If I don't do it no one else will.*

This kind of thinking goes completely against what the Bible teaches us about how we are meant to function alongside one another—each of us bringing different gifts. These verses from 1 Corinthians describe a body that has many parts, each part working together with the others. One part of the body can't take on all the responsibilities of the other parts. All parts are needed, and all parts are necessary.

> *If the whole body were an eye, where would the sense of hearing be? If the whole body were an ear, where would the sense of smell be? But in fact God has placed the parts in the body, every one of them, just as he wanted them to be. If they were all one part, where would the body be? As it is, there are many parts, but one body.*
>
> *1 Corinthians 12: 17–19 NIV*

In its simplest form, the truth I needed to rehearse was this: *If I don't do it, someone else will eventually step in.* If I don't do it, someone else will pick up the responsibility. If it doesn't get done, it doesn't get done. Whichever way, I needed to learn that even without me, it's all going to be okay.

Lie #2: If I don't do it, it must mean I am a bad person

This one was more painful for me and cut much deeper. This lie took me a lot longer to uncover and it was hard for me to voice it when I did. I was completely unaware that I had spent much of my life truly believing that if I didn't say yes then I must be a bad person. If I don't do this or that to help then I must not be a good pastor, not a good friend, sister, wife, mother, or daughter. Good people are supposed to help other people—right? Good people turn up. Good people say yes. Good people do everything they can. At least that's what I had convinced myself.

I believed I was somehow a bad person if I couldn't deliver on this 'Christian expectation' to say the right thing, be full of compassion, be quick to step up and counsel, pray and offer support. It wasn't helped by the trap of comparison—seeing other pastors, other leaders, other people who appeared to have it all together. I often compared myself to leaders around me who seemed to be able to consistently say yes. I also compared my needs with the things others needed and somehow concluded that their needs were more legitimate than mine. So, I pushed aside my need, whether that was rest, space, or quiet, and I would offer to help knowing full well I had absolutely no capacity to do so.

This message that not being able to do it all meant I was not a 'good' Christian came at me from every angle—even when reading the Bible. For years I'd looked at the early church described in Acts and had focussed on the fact that they sold all they had to give to one another. Many times throughout the Bible we are taught to look after the orphans, the widows, and the hungry. It is an intrinsic Christian act to help the needy— and so it should be! Of course we should help the needy. It's what Jesus would have done, isn't it? Or would he? It's easy to conclude that he healed everyone who came his way. He was available to everyone all the time and he had unlimited capacity.

It was a revelation to me that Jesus didn't in fact, do it all. Jesus gave more time to some than to others. A few even died while waiting for him to meet their needs! He didn't even prioritise every need—in fact, when the disciples complained about the extravagant outpouring by Mary, he chastised them. Their criticism was that the money was not spent on the poor. "But the poor you will always have with you," was his reply. On another occasion, crowds had gathered to hear Jesus preach, but he chose to go to another location, leaving them all behind on the shore!

Jesus didn't 'do it all', yet he was God, and he was good! He acted according to the season he was in, and what his Father was doing, rather than what people expected him to do. We see this shift in his focus during the later season of his ministry where there is a move away from the healing and miracles, to releasing the disciples and preparing them for his crucifixion.

For myself, it was my expectation of what I perceived a 'good' Christian to be that left me feeling like I often fell short. It left me believing that I was a 'bad' person because I couldn't deliver in the way I thought I should as a Christian. I needed to understand the season of ministry and life that I was in—and I needed to prioritise what God was asking me to do.

It wasn't until the lie was uncovered that I began to understand the guilt I had carried all my life. I had equated *doing* good with *being* good. Somehow, I had connected being good with doing good works. I had believed this since I was very young. I was the little person at church who did everything. I was on every team from the early age of eleven. I was serving in the under-fives, because helping wasn't just a good thing to do—in my mind, it *made me* good.

Our goodness is in Christ. We are in Christ, and he is good; therefore we are good. Not because of anything we do or do not do, but because we are *in him*. If we look at Ephesians 3, we read that we were saved by grace when we believed, and we can't take any credit for this. It is his righteousness, not ours—and that, we can't work for. Adam and Eve hadn't even started looking after the Garden when God said, "It is *very good*." Not just 'good' like all that God had created, but 'very good' in his eyes.

Until this realisation dawned on me, I lived with a constant pit in my stomach and a lump in my throat. "If I don't do it, then that must mean I'm a bad person," was often the cause of internal anxiety when I was approached to do something I knew I didn't have the capacity to do. I even went through a time when the sound of my phone ringing or the alert of a text message would send me into a panic attack. I would be awake all night, worried that I couldn't do whatever the person was going to ask me to do. An unrelenting burden that I should be able to pull off what others needed me to do weighed on my shoulders—even if logically and practically there were plenty of reasons why I couldn't. It was a burden that didn't resemble the lightness that Jesus taught about in the gospel of Matthew, and it certainly wasn't at all easy-breezy like the yoke (Matthew 11:30). Additionally, all of this didn't even take into account the times when I just plain didn't want to do the things that were asked of me!

Both of these lies only confirmed and solidified the belief that underpinned it all. "*If I don't do it no one else will*" and "*If I do say no then it makes me a bad person*," therefore I have no choice but to concede that *I must be responsible for everything.* I learnt that as long as this narrative was repeatedly running in my mind, then it was ruling my every behaviour! I had relinquished control, and I recognised it was keeping me trapped in habits that were no longer good for me.

For me, this shifted in a single moment of ministry when a visiting preacher placed his hand on my head and said through the microphone, "Your daddy is proud of you, and you don't have to try anymore." I just broke. It was the realisation that there was nothing I needed to 'do' for God to be proud of who I was. A weight lifted. I didn't need to try any more. Now I was able to begin rewriting the narrative in my mind.

Rewriting the Narrative

You may have heard or read information about how the formation of habits creates neural pathways in our brains. In the same way that travelling your car or bike along the same unsealed path over and over again will forge grooves along that pathway, our brains do the same with the messages that are communicated frequently. Have you noticed that when you ride your bike back over the grooves in that path, the wheels of the bike automatically slip down into them as it travels along the familiar path? It is just like that with the repetitive thoughts in our brains. As the neural impulses travel along those familiar paths, they automatically follow the same pathway each time, reinforcing the thought, habit, or behaviour. It's like the real-life version of *The Wheels on the Bus*—they go round and round, round and round. "The wheels on the bus go round and round all day long!" And yes! The song too, gets stuck going round and round in our heads—all day long. You're welcome!

This is why we can brush our teeth, drive our car, and get ourselves dressed without concentrating. We have repeated these activities so often that our minds and our bodies do it automatically. This is also why lies can become so embedded in our thinking that they dictate our behaviours without us even realising it. We have essentially hardwired our brains to believe them. The good news is that our brains are wonderfully complex creations and they *can* be rewired. Dr Caroline Leaf gives us this assurance: "If the brain can get worse by constantly focusing on the problem, then the brain can get better by understanding how to eliminate and replace the problem."[3]

It wasn't until God shifted the blockage in my heart and revealed something deeper—that nothing I do or don't do can change the fact that he is proud of me—that I finally embraced the truth. *He sees me as good.* I was fifteen years into my ministry journey, but now I could begin to alter the pathways, put an end to the repetition, and rewrite the narrative, creating new tracks for the wheels of my life to travel along.

Protecting the Borders

I've always loved airports. One of my proudest accomplishments is still the time I flew unaccompanied, as a child, all the way to London. My parents were already over there, and I was to join them from New Zealand for the school holidays. At age thirteen,

---

3 **Leaf, C.** *Switch On Your Brain: The Key to Peak Happiness, Thinking, and Health.* Baker Academic, Div of Baker Publishing Group, 2022.

I was too old for an airline chaperone so I ventured out on my own—I couldn't have been happier with my predicament. I even had an eight-hour stopover in Singapore where I was left to explore the vast airport all by myself. Whether I am travelling somewhere, or going to farewell or welcome other travellers, I love being there. I even love watching television shows about the comings and goings at airports.

We have some very strict customs and border control laws in our country, and as I watch the border control television shows, it always astounds me what people try to bring in. So many people bring prohibited and even non-prohibited items that they fail to declare. That is definitely not me! When I travel and go through the border checks, I am an over-declaring traveller. I declare all the things I need to and also all the things I don't need to. I just panic when I get to the airport staffer who is doing the checking. I start showing the gum I am chewing, the candy in the bag, and all the gifts I have purchased. I confess everything!

I am thankful that I live in a nation that wants to protect its borders from things that threaten it. I am thankful for systems at our airports and shipping ports that test and approve anything that is entering our country. I'm thankful that they don't just let everything in.

But I have to admit that it seems I am far less vigilant at protecting the borders of my own heart and mind. I wonder what thoughts are present at my border that need to be declared before I allow them to enter. Could I stop a thought before entry and ask, "What business do you have here?"

I wonder if some thinking has slipped in unchecked at the borders of your mind? We are encouraged in Romans 12:2 to test and approve our thinking against what God's will is for us. Does our thinking align with his will? Do we ultimately believe—in our hearts—that God sees us as good? Do we realise God's approval is already on us?

If you, too, have been believing the lie that *doing* good equates to *being* good, it's time to realign your heart to the heart of God. What other lies have you been believing? Let the Holy Spirit show you any thoughts that are not in alignment with God's truth about you. Romans 12:2 reassures us that we can be transformed by the renewing of our mind. When we let God minister into the deepest places of our hearts and take the time to identify the lies we have believed, it becomes a whole lot easier to rewrite the narrative.

VIII

Rewriting the Narrative

IT WAS ONE OF THE MOST BIZARRE CONVERSATIONS I HAVE HAD. A young person asked me for coffee to discuss some difficult things they were going through. They wanted my advice, so we sat down, ordered our hot drinks, and I listened as they explained the situation. After I had heard them tell of their predicament, I attempted to offer some thoughts—the advice they had asked for. With every word of wisdom, encouragement, relatable scenario, and scripture verse (I mean, I pulled out all the stops!)that came from my mouth, a *"Yeah, but . . ."* came from theirs.

"Yeah, but it will take too long."

"Yeah, but they said this . . ."

"Yeah, but that worked for them, it won't work for me."

"Yeah, but they won't believe me."

"Yeah, but I can't do that."

"Yeah, but I don't want to do that."

"Yeah, but I tried that and it didn't work."

I have never heard so many *yeah, buts* in one conversation, and I reflected on the meeting sadly, realising that as much as they might have wanted change, nothing was going to shift in their circumstance until they changed the way they thought about it *and* spoke about it.

But this is the way that running commentary works, doesn't it? Behaviour change is limited without a change in narrative. I too had some narrative-driven behaviours that needed some attention. For years I told myself that saying no to someone made me a bad person and as long as I kept believing that then I was trapped in a cycle of never being able to say anything other than *yes*—despite what that might mean for the other rightfully, high-prioritised things in my life.

If I was going to see real change, I had to learn that there was a deeper work that needed to take place, and it needed to start before the thinking and before the speaking. It started with my heart.

New Heart

There's some pretty clear advice about our heart in Proverbs 4:23 (NIV): "Above all else, guard your heart, for everything you do flows from it." We all have a physical heart—a small organ that we probably don't think about all that often and yet it plays an incredibly important role. The main job of the heart is to pump blood to every part of the body. The blood carries oxygen and all the vitamins, minerals, and nutrition that our body needs to move, think, grow and repair itself. The heart keeps us alive and causes the rest of our body to function. But this verse from Proverbs is not speaking about our physical heart. In fact, most of the time when the Bible refers to our 'heart', it is speaking about the innermost part of us that makes up who we are.

This verse emphasises the great significance of this seemingly insignificant part of us. Just like the physical heart, our spirit has an enormous role to play when it comes to how we function—because everything we do flows from our heart. The condition of our heart determines our thoughts, our speech, and our actions. Our heart determines who we become. For thoughts, speech and actions to change, there needs to be a change in the heart. Ultimately, what we need is a heart transplant. I am so grateful that one of the promises we receive through Christ when we surrender our lives to him is the promise of a new heart.

This means that anyone who belongs to Christ has become a new person. The old life is gone; a new life has begun!
2 Corinthians 5:17

Through Christ, the old Becs has gone. When the visiting speaker put his hand on my head and said, "Your daddy is proud of you and you don't have to try anymore," God ministered to the deepest places in my heart. I realised that I had been spending a lot of time and effort trying to work for the acceptance and approval of both God and others. I was trying to convince people, through my hard work, that I was 'good' and 'deserving' and 'worthy' of love. But on that day, a shift took place, and it wasn't because of anything I had done. It was as if God himself was doing open-heart surgery on me. He transformed the inner parts of my being and made me new.

While that heart transplant moment was life-changing—in an instant, I knew I was made new—the process of renewal is something we have to be constantly attuned to. Heart work is continuous, and we need to have regular 'check-ups' to assess the condition of our heart. We must frequently ask ourselves, "What is going on in my heart? Why am I responding in this way? Is there something deeper going on here that I need to listen to?"

I also became aware of the need for my thinking and my words to catch up with the heart transformation. Now I began to notice how often I thought: *Yeah, but they really need help and there is no one else who can do it*, or even, *Yeah, but I have time on my day off so it's no big deal if I squeeze it in*. My heart renewal opened my eyes to the many habitual responses that were simply not helpful or healthy. I came to see that if I was going to change my automatic reactions then I had to re-write the 'yeah buts' both in my thinking and my speaking—which would eventually lead to a re-write in my doing.

New Thinking

Following the great exodus out of Egypt, the Lord led Moses and the Israelites to Mount Sinai. In Exodus, we read the account of Moses on the mountain communing with God while he receives all of God's laws and commandments for the people. Meanwhile, the Israelites at the foot of the mountain are worshipping a golden calf that they have built. Listen to what God says to Moses about this:

> *They have quickly turned from the way I commanded them; they have made for themselves an image of a calf. They have bowed down to it, sacrificed to it, and said, "Israel, these are your gods, who brought you up from the land of Egypt."*
>
> *Exodus 32:8*

The Israelites had gone back to worshipping the gods of the land where they'd been held captive. They were willingly enslaving themselves once more to the old habits and old ways. When you don't understand your complete freedom, you will believe any lie that tries to convince you that the past you have been freed from is better than the new land you are being promised. The Israelites had convinced themselves that the gods that held them captive were the gods that could set them free. They believed the lie that going back to their slavery was better for them, and because they believed the lie, they were not able to break free from their slave mentality. The same can be very true in our lives. For every thought still holding us captive, there is a lie that we have believed. As long as we keep believing it we will never be truly free.

For so long, I had believed a lie—and lived as though it were true. To experience lasting freedom and change in my life, I had to have a new way of thinking. In the same way that God had renewed my heart, I needed him to renew my mind.

Romans 12:2 (CSB) describes it like this:

Do not be conformed to this age, but be transformed by the renewing of your mind, so that you may discern what is the good, pleasing, and perfect will of God.

Often, we think that we have no choice but to let any old thought in. We forget that we can set up our own border control, just like at the airport, and decline or accept those thoughts upon entry. Another translation of that same verse reads:

Do not conform to the pattern of this world, but be transformed by the renewing of your mind. Then you will be able to test and approve what God's will is—his good, pleasing and perfect will.

Romans 12:2 NIV

In other words, you don't have to allow every thought access to your life. This passage states clearly that we are to *test* and *approve* anything trying to gain access to our thinking.

Your freedom begins in your heart and mind before it can take place anywhere else. Where in your thoughts do you need to make some changes? What are you allowing to take up residence in your heart and mind that you have neither tested nor approved?

In my experience, I have learnt that our thoughts are deeply connected to our speech. At first, it might feel a bit intangible to consider changing your thoughts—it's a lot harder than changing a car tyre for example. You cannot lay hold of your thoughts or physically see them so to change them feels hard to grasp. However, the evidence of your thoughts is in our speech, and because our speech derives from our thinking, I believe one of the fastest ways to change our thinking is to consciously change the way we speak.

The connection between our heart, our thinking, and our speaking has been understood since the beginning of time. In Paul's second letter to the Corinthians, he writes:

> *It is written: "I believed; therefore I have spoken." Since we have that same spirit of faith, we also believe and therefore speak . . .*
>
> 2 Corinthians 4:13 NIV

New Narrative

Remember that conversation we started about the neural pathways in our brains? We talked about the bicycle wheels that travel over and over the same path, creating furrows or grooves that make it easier for the wheels to travel in those same hollows each time. The little dirt pathway, in time, becomes a highway. So it is with our neural pathways. God, in his wisdom and grace, created our brains in such a way that they can be rewired and our negative, damaging thoughts can be replaced by a new narrative.

Caroline Leaf speaks about how simply having hope can set our brain on a positive pathway:

> "Thoughts are real, physical things that occupy mental real estate. Moment by moment, every day, you are changing the structure of your brain through your thinking. When we

hope, it is an activity of the mind that changes the structure of our brain in a positive and normal direction."[4]

We have to carve out a new pathway. We must be deliberate, decisive, and conscious—and we can do that with the help of our words. I might not *feel* like I have much control over my thoughts right now, but one thing I can control is how I speak.

I like Caroline Leaf's phrase, "Frame your world with your words."[5] It reminds me of 2 Corinthians 4:13: "I believe, therefore I speak." There is a progression here: Establish the belief, correct the lies, and then speak the truth.

I learnt how I could do this through working with my counsellor. We took one of the lies I had been telling myself: *If I say no, that makes me a bad person.* Then we put it under the spotlight and began to dissect it to establish whether it was true or a lie.

My counsellor asked, "Is that true? Are you a bad person?" Then he said, "Let's look for some evidence that supports that you are a good person." He helped me to list everything that shows I am a good person. I must admit I found this to be incredibly awkward and it was very hard to begin with—it must have felt a bit like pulling teeth to him. We listed things such as: I look after and love my children, I look after and love my husband, I help people in my job, I have lots of friends, I carry out acts of kindness toward others, and I encourage people with my words.

4 Leaf, C. *Switch On Your Brain: The Key to Peak Happiness, Thinking, and Health*. Baker Academic, Div of Baker Publishing Group, 2022.

5 Leaf, C. *Who Switched Off My Brain?: Controlling Toxic Thoughts and Emotions*. Improv Limited, 2009

Once we had painstakingly created this list of evidence, he said to me, "And maybe you're not just good but you are also wise. After all, it is wise to put in boundaries. And now that we have established that you are a good and wise person, perhaps it's then okay to say no."

The narrative *can* change. It is no longer truthful to think that if I say no, then I am a bad person—I need to change that. It is also important to weigh those lies against the truth of God's word. The Bible serves as a foundational benchmark for truth, providing clarity and guidance in a world often filled with deception and confusion. It takes a deliberate and ongoing process of taking our thoughts to the Word and consistently searching to uncover God's truth. We must regularly ask ourselves, "What does Scripture say about this?"

We can fast-track this process not only by going to God's word whenever we need to challenge a lie, but also by staying in God's word regularly. The practices of everyday reading, and meditating on and memorising scripture, will help tremendously in developing our ability to distinguish truth from lies. Ultimately, the transformative power of God's word renews our hearts, aligns our thoughts with his truth, and enables us to live in freedom and authenticity.

My counsellor and I came up with two new narratives based on the lies we had untangled. To counter the lie that "Saying no makes me a bad person," we decided on: "*I am a good and wise person, and it's okay to say no, just because.*" For my second lie, "I am responsible for everything," we decided on the new narrative, "*I am not responsible for everything.*" And here is where it became even more uncomfortable for me—I was under instructions to look at myself in the mirror and repeat those new narratives three to five times at least twice each day.

*"I am a good and wise person and it's okay to say **no**, just because. I am **not** responsible for everything.*

*I am a good and wise person and it's okay to say **no**, just because. I am **not** responsible for everything.*

*I am a good and wise person and it's okay to say **no**, just because. I am **not** responsible for everything."*

The beautiful thing about God's word is that it is written to teach us who God is, and in discovering who he is, we also discover who we are. When his word is written on our hearts and our new narratives are grounded deeply in scripture, we become aligned with God's nature and God's purpose for us.

Encouraged by a good friend, I began to declare biblical truths over myself during my prayer times each day. Every morning and every night I would find a space where nobody could interrupt me, and I would speak these declarations out loud:

I am a child of God.

I am loved.

I am protected.

I am blessed.

I am made for a purpose.

I am filled with the power of the Holy Spirit.

I am forgiven and redeemed.

I am never alone.

I am fully and completely known.

I am more than a conqueror.

Honestly? I didn't always feel like doing it. Those words did not always feel true—I wasn't always convinced when I was saying them. On those days, I simply had to speak out of hope and expectation. I had to decide that while I may not feel it, I was still going to speak it.

New Habits

When it comes to a heart transformation, we can change our thinking and we can change our language, but there comes a time when we also have to see change come in our actions. One thing should lead to another, but we do need to make some deliberate choices to ultimately live the free life God intended.

The writer of Philippians encourages us to "keep putting into practice" what we are being taught.

> *And now, dear brothers and sisters, one final thing. Fix your thoughts on what is true, and honorable, and right, and pure, and lovely, and admirable. Think about things that are excellent and worthy of praise. **Keep putting into practice** all you learned and received from me—everything you heard from me and saw me doing. Then the God of peace will be with you.* Philippians 4:8-9 NLT

When we continually put into practice what we are learning, it becomes a pattern, forming that behaviour into a habit. Our habits are the everyday things we do without even thinking. Sometimes we begin those habits out of choice, and other times we don't even realise we've developed them.

Habits often make up parts of our daily routine, and those routines help us to get through our list of tasks quickly and effortlessly because they allow us to switch to autopilot. We don't need to think intentionally about what we are doing because the actions have become automatic—remember, it's a neural pathway thing. Habits and daily routines are good because they help us save our creative capacity for more valuable tasks throughout the day. Where our habits will trip us up, is when they are not helpful, but detrimental, to us. Habits like saying *yes* without considering the cost, jumping in to take over when your child is attempting a task independently, even saying, "I'm great, thanks," when that is far from reality.

If your habits lead you toward decisions that continue to imprison you, may I encourage you to begin living your life less out of those habits and more out of intent? Determine now that nothing is left to chance, that you are living mindful of your actions, your decisions, your responses, and the habits that are out to trip you up. We can ask ourselves: What habits do I need to change? What default response am I giving that is causing me to remain stuck?

On a practical level, this might mean that you need to pre-determine a new set of responses. It is the on-the-spot demand that trips us up and causes us to go straight back to the old habits. We get caught off guard and struggle to think quickly enough to come up with something new. But if we could take the time to write down a new set of responses—ones that line up with the new narrative—then we have something prepared and tucked into our back pocket to pull out when the moment arises.

When a song that you grew up singing comes onto the radio, it is automatically familiar, isn't it? You know the ones I am talking about—all the songs that you listened to constantly, on repeat. The thing about music is that even twenty years on, you still know all the words, you can jump right in and start singing, and as those lyrics come flooding back so do all the feelings. It's all so familiar—like a comforting nostalgic experience.

The same is true with these lies we have been talking about. Even though we have done the heart-work to overcome them, something can happen in our day to trigger a reminder of that negative thought, and all of a sudden it feels familiar. The previous narrative begins to play again and it's so easy to slip back into that old groove we used to travel. After that, it often doesn't take much for old patterns to form once more. I am not perfect at this. I still get it wrong. I still have to have constant conversations with my husband so he can help me to unpack my behaviours and we can discuss whether I'm doing too much. *Is it me who needs to be the one doing it? Do I need to reach out and ask for help?* The first step is to recognise the lie. Then you can acknowledge the thought and make a conscious decision to stop pushing play or pressing repeat. Finally, speak with hope and expectation.

IX

Out of Egypt

A N ELEPHANT STANDS, STRONG AND POWERFUL. TIED AROUND HIS ankle is a small rope—too small to restrain such a massive creature, and yet the elephant never attempts to break free. It's a strange picture. Why doesn't the elephant just walk away? He could. And why don't his captors use a sturdier rope to secure such an animal? They know that the elephant, having been tied by that same tether since he was a younger, much smaller elephant, does not realise that he has grown far more powerful than that which restrains him. He does not know that he has outgrown the strength of his captors, or that with very little effort he could be free.

We can live our whole lives like that elephant. Free, but never taking a step into that freedom. The Israelites lived at the end of an 'elephant rope' in the wilderness. They had been freed from slavery, but they didn't understand the greatness of their identity.

The book of Exodus tells their freedom story. For around four hundred years, God's people had been living in slavery in the land of Egypt under the iron rule of Pharaoh. Then God sent a deliverer—a man called Moses; a Hebrew who had grown up as an Egyptian prince—and designated to him the task of leading the campaign for Israel's freedom. Summoning his courage, Moses petitioned Pharaoh to let his people go. When Pharaoh refused, God sent ten plagues to sweep through the land. God was intent on seeing his people set free!

Interestingly, when studying these plagues, I learnt that for every affliction, there was an associated Egyptian god. God wasn't so much coming against the people, the land, or even Pharoah, he was destroying the spiritual entities that kept the people in bondage. We read, "I will execute judgment against all the gods of Egypt" (Exodus 12:12). We must understand that when God delivered the Israelites from slavery and led them to their freedom, he was giving them more than just their physical liberty. He was setting them free from every power and authority that kept them oppressed and enslaved.

The shocking miracle of the Nile being turned to blood alluded to the Egyptian god *Hapi*, a 'water-bearer' whose bloodstream was the Nile. The plague of frogs came against the goddess of fertility, *Heket*, who had the head of a frog. The plague of gnats was a sign against the Egyptian god *Geb*, who ruled over the dust of the earth. The swarms of flies alluded to the fly god, *Khepri*, who had the head of a fly . . . and so on, until the Lord brought a plague of darkness over the face of the sun god *Ra*, the most revered god after Pharoah, and finally, a plague of death against Pharoah himself, the 'ultimate power of Egypt' (Exodus 7:14–11:10).

With every plague, Almighty God, the God of Abraham, Isaac and Jacob, showed the Israelites that he was above every other god. They belonged to him, and he was more powerful than anything they would encounter in the land of their captivity. God wasn't just setting them free from physical slavery—he was setting them free from the fears, the threats, and the mindsets they had become accustomed to.

You would think that after such an obvious display of the superiority of their God, and the great lengths he was prepared to go to for them to be set free, that they would step confidently into their new life. And yet, even after the Israelites had been set free, they continually grumbled and complained against the Lord.

> *"Why didn't God let us die in comfort in Egypt where we had lamb stew and all the bread we could eat?"*
>
> *Exodus 16:3*

> *The people grumbled at Moses, saying, "What are we to drink?"*
>
> *Exodus 15:22-27*

In response, God in all his goodness gave them the miracle of daily manna and sent quails for meat (Exodus 16:1-7, 11-12). In Exodus 17, we read that God provided water. Every need was met. They needn't have been worried about provisions.

Just like the elephant with the rope around its leg, the Israelites were physically free but still bound by their slave mentality. They were free from captivity, but they still thought like slaves instead of like beloved children of the Most High God.

91

When God delivered his people, he desired to bring them into complete freedom. Friend, he has the same desire for you and me today. God's intention is not that we would live weighed down, chained and held captive by our past mindsets. His intention is for us to live in freedom. Free from the weight. Free from the burden. Free from unrealistic expectations. And when I say free, I mean *completely free*. Not half-free, partially free, or somewhat free. Completely free!

For years, I felt trapped in false responsibility. It was a self-imposed cycle, a never-ending loop that I couldn't switch off. I often felt like a hamster on a wheel, running, running, running endlessly, never slowing down, and never quite feeling brave enough to jump off. I often asked myself, *Will it always feel this heavy? Am I always going to feel like I'm out of my depth? Will I ever not feel trapped in a rhythm I'm not content with?* My life was like an uncomfortable song where I couldn't quite catch the melody. I couldn't live with it, but I couldn't see how not to live with it. I was in a state of constant unease, and I was afraid that this was it, that I would have to live out the rest of my days feeling exhausted and under a heavy load.

This was more than having a schedule that was out of control. For years I tried to solve the feeling inside by lessening the demands on the calendar, by delegating responsibilities. But the feeling remained. I kept finding myself back in the same old cycle. Why? Because the real issue wasn't physical—it was at a deeper level. I needed to realise, like the Israelites, that I was no longer held in bondage. Christ had triumphed over every spirit of oppression.

I wonder how many of us are walking around free but still acting as if we are trapped? This can be true in any area of our lives. We can be free from a broken relationship but still plagued by bitterness and unforgiveness—trapped in a prison of resentment. We can be free from our old life of sin, but still held captive by shame and condemnation. Maybe by God's grace we have been set free from the need for perfection, but we are still chained in our thinking by pride and the need for control. That last one? That was me. I knew on one level that I was already perfect and complete in Christ, but I couldn't shake the spirit of perfectionism. It is one thing to be set free, it is another thing to live in freedom daily.

Living with the burden of responsibility was not the way God had designed me to live. I needed to be reminded that I really could live faithful to the call that God had placed on my life without the heaviness and burden. It's not often obvious how much freedom we have. Like the elephant, we look at the tether holding us in place and fail to see how easy it would be to step into the wide-open spaces before us. It's like being locked in an escape room. We can spend hours feeling claustrophobic, looking for clues to help us unlock the door and free us, only to discover that the location of the key was obvious all along.

The truth is that life can be cryptic and confusing. It can seem like the key to our freedom is always elusive—no wonder we get disheartened and discouraged. We forget that Christ has already set us free. He's already done the heavy lifting. He's broken the bondage and flung wide the doors! This is a life-changing realisation. In the Bible, we read:

For freedom, Christ sets us free. Stand firm and don't submit again to the yolk of slavery.

Galatians 5:1

Paul, the writer of this letter to the Galatian church, is urging them not to get caught back up in the slavery mindset that God had already freed them from. Let's not be like people who spend an hour in an escape room only to realise the key was in their pocket all along! God has freedom for us! We *can* do life differently. It doesn't always have to be this way.

Do you feel trapped by your endless round of responsibilities? Does it feel impossible to get off the hamster wheel? Just like the Israelites, it is going to take some deep heart work for us to embrace the freedom God has brought us. You can be a wife, a mum, a friend, a minister, and still live free from the burden of carrying it all.

X

I am not a Control Freak, I Just Like to be in Control

IF THERE IS ONE THING I STRUGGLE WITH AS A MOTHER, IT IS allowing my children into the kitchen to help me cook or bake. I am going to be honest here so remember our agreement about the no judgement thing! I don't just *not* enjoy it, I hate it. It's nightmare stuff for me. All I can think about is the mess. It's out of control. Everything, everywhere. As soon as my boys ask, "Mum, can we do some baking?", I begin to picture flour on every surface and dishes exploding out of the sink. Mess, mess, and more mess. And don't even get me started on the actual baking itself; I cannot just be the encouraging observer, nor am I the coach who stands on the sidelines and gently directs. I am the coach who yells and screams and has to hold herself back from running onto the pitch to take over! I almost have to sit on my hands to stop myself from grabbing the mixer, the spoon, and the ingredients and just doing it all myself! It would be so much easier, tidier, and probably more edible too.

For years I have told myself that I am not a control freak. But who am I kidding? If our Saturday plans change at the last minute, even just a little, I have to take myself off to do some deep breathing exercises before I can come back and pretend that I like the new plan and that I'm cool to just 'go with the flow'. Please tell me I am not the only one!

Our Desire For Certainty

Control: I like the Oxford dictionary's definition of 'control' as a verb. To *be in control* is to "determine the behaviour or supervise the running of a person or thing." That sounds a little better than the noun: "the power to influence or direct people's behaviour or the course of an event." The former makes me sound less like a control freak! Truthfully though, in the same way that one might use a 'control' in a scientific experiment, maintaining a sense of control in my world is all about measuring and taking into account the factors that might affect outcomes.

If we can keep all the variables constant, then we can better ensure that everything will remain 'okay'. If we can be the one to hold all the balls, then we can be the one to make sure none of them drop. As humans, we use control as a way of calming chaos, finding peace, and bringing a level of predictability to life. Being in control helps us build security and safety.

Tony Robbins speaks about the six human needs that drive the decisions we make: certainty, uncertainty or spontaneity, significance, connection or love, growth, and a sense of contribution.[6] He highlights that behind every behaviour, emotion and reaction, behind our successes and our failures,

6 Robbins, T. 2023. "Discover The 6 Human Needs". https://www.tonyrobbins.com/mind-meaning/do-you-need-to-feel-significant/

is a human need that we are prioritising—and we all prioritise them differently. We each choose to put some needs ahead of others based on our personalities, our childhood experiences, life's events, and circumstances.

It didn't take me long to figure out which of the six needs *I* was prioritising. This control freak is all about *certainty*. It makes me feel safe and secure to know that things are either in my control or someone else's. The worst feeling is the thought that no one has control! I need to know that I am safe. That my life is safe. My future is safe. That my happy little world is safe. This is not necessarily a bad thing. It is a reflection of my personality. It's true of most of us. Discovering certainty was my highest need helped me to see that particular relationships in my life were providing me with my other needs for connection, love, belonging, and security.

In my marriage, I feel safe. My husband has this incredible ability to remember information. Not necessarily important stuff, but if you are heading to a quiz night Steve is the guy you want on your team. He just knows and retains stuff, and he also always knows what to do. He has disaster plans for every scenario. If we are on a boat, at a restaurant or in an airport, within the first five minutes he has already worked out our escape route if the worst were to happen. He is strong, he is capable. He makes me feel safe and certain.

As a daughter, I feel secure. My dad knows how to do anything! And if he doesn't know he will figure it out. He just seems to know how things work, and I trust him completely. He has always made me feel loved and valued. The way he treats me shows me that I am important to him. I am confident when I am near him. I look to him for direction, assurance, and security.

Understanding this need for certainty has helped me to recognise some of my negative patterns of behaviour. As a young mother, I chose order and environmental organisation over quality time with my children—it just made me feel secure to have everything neat and tidy. I was *that* mum who, instead of enjoying playing with her child, would follow around after him picking up the toys and reorganising the Lego. To this day I still often miss the first half of our Friday night movie time because I just have to clean up the kitchen before I come and join in the family fun.

Surrendering Control

Often I let my need to control my environment trump the greater needs in my life. For many years, control and that desire for certainty seemed to shout the loudest and would often drown out my other needs. Needs like rest, family time, fun, enjoyment, self-care, connecting with God, connecting with others. All of those greater needs weren't getting a voice because I simply needed to prioritise control.

Letting go of control in my day-to-day life felt like a losing battle. I didn't want to be a control freak, but neither did I want to be at odds with the part of me that likes order. When we look at the Bible, we can see that God also likes order. He brings storms to rest, he orders the days and nights and seasons, and our bodies are made with systems and structures.

He is a God of certainty. Seedtime and harvest, day and night will never cease (Genesis 8:22). Perhaps our love of control is in some way an expression of God's Spirit within us, bringing peace, order and certainty wherever we go.

If Jesus is the perfect representation of God, then we have to acknowledge that there's a level of unpredictability with God. There were many times when Jesus flipped things on their head. He wasn't tied to a preset plan. He was able to be spontaneous, and he was comfortable about it—much to other people's annoyance.

He didn't take the most efficient route to Jerusalem—he decided to go through Samaria.

He stopped to speak with the woman at the well.

He saw Zaccheaus in the tree and put the whole trip on hold while he went in for dinner at his house.

He was on his way to heal someone, but he stopped to minister to the woman with the issue of blood.

He defended his disciples when they picked grain on the sabbath.

He didn't bother with the ritual washing of hands.

In short, nothing seemed set in stone with Jesus. He wasn't 'out of control', but he wasn't a control freak. He was fully submitted and surrendered to heaven. Ultimately, he was able to say, "Not my will but yours," when it really mattered.

It stretches my faith to have to let go and let God have control. To let him work in the way he wants to work. To lean into his timing rather than insist on my own. To submit to his plans when they don't fit the blueprint I have ordered. Sometimes it takes all my self-discipline not to dive in and start telling the God of the universe how to run this planet!

The reassuring thing is that God isn't asking us to be all-or-nothing. One of the fruits of the spirit is self-control. God planned for us to partner with him to bring order, peace and safety to our world and those around us. But he also calls us to submit our agenda and to hold our plans and our desires with an open hand. When we let God take charge, he finds a way to give us the desires of our heart. We don't always need to know what's going on or be the one to dictate how everything gets done.

Our oldest boy is at the stage where he wants to know all the things. He wants to be part of all the adult conversations and be privy to everything that's going on. You could say he has major FOMO. He loves to put his little nose into everything. If something we say catches his attention and curiosity, he perks up and says, "Wait, what?!", then comes charging over to look and see what he's been missing. Steve and I find ourselves constantly saying to him, "Nosy parker, get your nose out, it's not your business."

Sometimes I think I am like my teenage son. I have probably pulled a "Wait, what?" on God more times than I care to admit. I wonder how often God wants to tell me to get my nose out of his business! Maybe I need to surrender control and simply trust him, rather than needing to have all my ducks lined up.

For many years, trust was hard for me. To trust someone else meant I had to let go of the outcome. It meant I had to be okay not knowing. Trusting God meant I might never know the answers. But there is something I have learnt on this journey, and I hope you will be able to know this truth too: He is trustworthy. You *can* surrender control—because he is trustworthy.

As believers, we are all here on earth, saying, "Wait, what? What's going on here, Lord? And what are you doing over there?" It's easy to get all up in a whole bunch of things that just aren't our responsibility, and God is like, "Get your nose out of it. Just trust that I've got it sorted."

Are there things in your life that help you feel safe and secure? Let's celebrate these! But let's also ask God to show us the areas of our lives where we are unable to release control. Let's trust him for our sense of safety and security. When we let God—and sometimes others—take the reins, we may just find that our little world is still okay after all.

XI

Waving the White Flag

R EMEMBER THE ESCAPE ROOM SCENARIO—THE TINY ROOM, THE complex puzzles, the locks and keys? However, one thing I didn't mention was that at any point you can press a button and request a clue. I have played the Escape Room game several times with different groups of people, and I always find it very interesting that whenever we come up against something that has us well and truly baffled, all the different personalities come out to play. Some people are way too quick to press the clue button and want all the help they can get. Then there are the ones who refuse, under any circumstances, to push that button. They're the ones who are most frustrating to play with. They will not admit defeat. They will not concede weakness.

For those of us who pride ourselves on being capable, strong and resilient, it is a big step to recognise that we can't do it all. What's worse is when we find out that not only can we not do it all but we can't do *any of it*. It's the point where we have no choice but to wave the white flag—we *need* help.

Moses got to that point. After months of trying to fix the Israelites' problems, tend to their complaints and intercede on their behalf, he finally snapped. Moses had what I call a 'holy meltdown' before the Lord. "I can't do it anymore. These people are too much for me," says Moses (Numbers 11:14). And no wonder. Moses had led the Israelites out of Egypt and taken them into the wilderness en route to the Promised Land, but instead of hearing their gratitude or enthusiasm for what lay ahead, it had been a year of listening to their complaining, moaning, and constant grumbling.

I get you, Moses, I have had my fair share of holy meltdowns! "That's it, I've had enough! I can't carry this on my own!" Have you found yourself there too?

"I can't carry my teenager on my own."

"I can't carry my marriage on my own."

"I can't carry the financial strain on my own."

"I can't carry our family dysfunction on my own."

"It's too much for me."

We have all been there in one way or another.

In truth, while it may not feel like it at the time, this is a good place to get to. It is uncomfortable and we don't like being in this position, but I have learnt that this is the best position to be in if we are ever to let go of all the responsibility. To live free of false responsibility and self-reliance, we each have to go through the process of realising, *I just can't.* Each of us will have a 'wave the white flag' moment of surrender—the moment when we admit that we have come to the end of ourselves, and we are ready to hand it all over to God.

The thought of dropping it all can be almost unbearable because our usual *modus operandi* is, "I've got this." It's like arriving home from the supermarket with a boot full of groceries. We arrive home, we open the boot, we take one look at the bags and think, *Yep, I can do this on my own.* Then we take one look at the distance from car to house and think, *in fact, I can also do it in one go.* Then we proceed to overload ourselves ridiculously in our attempt to carry an entire boot load of groceries to the front door in one trip.

"Do you need some help, Honey?"

"No, I've got it."

"Are you sure? 'Cos it looks like you could do with some help."

"No, I'm good!"

Surrender requires us to trust God with what we can't carry, but it also requires opening ourselves up to getting help from others. And I am not sure which is harder. Waving the white flag involves putting ourselves at the mercy of others—which isn't easy when we are used to being the ones who carry the load.

Check out how God responds to Moses' cry for help:

> The Lord answered Moses, "Bring me seventy men from Israel known to you as elders and officers of the people. Take them to the tent of meeting ad have them stand there with you. Then I will come down and speak with you

there. I will take some of the Spirit who is on you and put
the Spirit on them. They will help you bear the burden of
the people, so that you do not have to bear it by yourself."

Numbers 11:16-18

Notice that God's response was not to dive in and fix the situation
for Moses. God responded by equipping and empowering others
to assist Moses. These people were not fundamentally different
to Moses; they carried the same spirit as he did. Effectively, they
were already there to help manage the load. This is important—
God never intended us to carry the whole burden by ourselves.
Carrying the whole load is an assumption we came up with all
on our own. We can feel like there's no one around to help. But
take another look. We are all surrounded by people we can call
on for help. These may be people from our community, our
neighbours, church friends or leaders, our colleagues, and even
trained professionals. But we must learn how to invite others
to help us.

When we've realised we can't do it anymore, when we've waved
the white flag, what next? It was one thing for me to say, "I can't
do it anymore," but it was another to know how to let go and let
other people do things for me. Here is what I learnt:

1. Start Small

Begin by asking for help with small, inconsequential tasks or
relatively insignificant situations. In other words, start with the
things you care least about. You might find these things a little
easier to let go of, so these can be a great starting point. As
you experience the freedom and benefit of allowing others to

carry some of the responsibility, you will gradually build your confidence in asking for help. Choose a specific area that is small enough that it won't send you into a panic at the thought of handing it over, but that would make a difference to you if someone were to lend a hand. Set some goals for yourself—go on, give yourself a box to tick, but this time the box is not one more thing for *you* to do, instead it is something you will ask *someone else* to do!

2. Identify a Safe Support System

Take some time to identify someone, or preferably a small group of people, you can trust. This is important because if you don't trust these people, you won't reach out to them. Knowing you have a *reliable* support system can make it so much easier to ask for help. Make sure you spend time on this. *Who in your world do you see as being reliable and dependable? Who has proven themselves to be trustworthy in another area? What type of people could offer you support or understanding?* You do not need to come up with a long list. It's okay to keep it small—especially if you are a leader. Do not feel obliged to let everyone in. Do not feel pressured to tell everyone everything—I recommend you don't, but what I do know is you need a handful of trusted people who you feel confident will turn up for you.

3. Say Yes to Offers

This was very hard for me. I didn't like the thought that I was putting people out. But what I had to realise is that what is true for me is most likely true for someone else too. For example, when I offer to assist someone, I genuinely mean it. I am offering because I am happy to help with their needs. If that's the case for me, then why should I not believe it would be the case when the roles are reversed? I learnt this the hard way.

I don't remember much about that day, or what led to it, but I do remember the excruciating pain. It started that afternoon—a stabbing pain through my lower abdomen. I took Panadol, I took Nurofen, and I tried a heat pack, but nothing would make it go away! It was as though I was going through stage four labour pains, except I wasn't in labour—I wasn't even pregnant. I went to bed that night, but I couldn't sleep. The more time went on, the worse the pain got.

At three o'clock in the morning, I finally woke my husband and told him I needed to go to the emergency room. We had the "What do we do?" conversation. Should we wake the boys and take them? They were still too young to leave at home alone. In the end, I insisted Steve should stay with them and I would drive myself. I did not see any other way.

That drive is up there with one of the worst and most difficult experiences of my life. As I watched the kilometres go by, I prayed and prayed that God would get me there faster. Somehow, I got to the hospital, found a parking spot, and made my way to the emergency room. Thankfully, the receptionist saw the state I was in and took me right on through. It took a dose of morphine and some other tiny pills to get my pain under control. After a myriad of tests, a night in the hospital, and some more of those tiny pills, I was sent home still not knowing what had caused the pain.

The following day, when my neighbour—a good friend of mine—found out that I had driven myself to the hospital at 3:00 a.m. in severe pain, boy was she mad at me! She could not believe that she and her husband were just two houses away, yet I hadn't called to ask them to drive me to the hospital. That was a wake-up call for me. It helped me realise that people *want* to help, and we need to let them.

We have to settle it in our hearts that it's okay to decide we are done! It's okay to admit you are empty, that you simply have nothing left in the tank—to wave the white flag. It's okay to admit it to yourself, and it's okay to admit it to others. And it's also okay not to drop everything immediately—you can start small. You could begin by asking a friend for a cuppa to share some of the mental load you are carrying. You could start by choosing just one thing you can put down and one way you can say yes to an offer of help. The truth is, small things really can make the biggest difference. With a few of these baby steps. perhaps you will begin to see that waving that little flag of surrender isn't so scary after all.

XII

Forgetting We
Need God

ONE NEW YEAR'S EVE WE WERE INVITED TO CELEBRATE AT A friend's house. Their backyard was the perfect place for a party: they had a swimming pool, fireworks, a firepit for toasting marshmallows, and the smell of a delicious barbeque already sizzling away. The chaos of having six families together was increasing, and just as the sun went down, our youngest son came frantically running toward us in tears. He had fallen off the trampoline and landed on his shoulder. It was obvious that he had broken his collarbone. Let's just say it put an abrupt end to our New Year's celebrations.

Two weeks after his initial x-ray, we went back to see the doctor to check on progress. The doctor explained that his collarbone was only just beginning to knit back together—it was healing, but we still needed to take it easy. He urged us to be even more careful because although our son was no longer in pain and had no need for a sling, his collarbone was still weak. "Without the sling to remind him of this weakness, it may be easier for him to fall, or collide with someone, or bump it, causing the collarbone to be re-broken," the doctor explained. In other words, the slightest knock could send him back to square one. We learnt that, statistically, the collarbone carries the highest risk of being re-broken, and the reason for that is because even if we think it's better—it looks better, it feels better, there's no cast, no sling and no reminder of brokenness—*it's still weak!* We can presume it's strong, but it's not.

I can't help but think that you and I are like that broken collarbone. From the outside, we become very good at making our lives look strong, with no signs of brokenness. We are so good at keeping up appearances that we become experts at looking and even feeling stronger than we are. When that happens, we are depending on our ability to hold it all together.

In my walk with God, I have noticed that I find it much easier to stay connected to him in seasons when I know I need him. When I am without strength, I can easily recognise my need for God. I cry out to him in my desperation. I dig deep because I have no other choice—I know I am nothing without him.

It is in that place of desperation that we find Asa, one of the kings of Judah. In 2 Chronicles, we read that he was up against the Cushites, who who had an army twice the size of his. He was kidding himself if he thought he could defeat them by his own might, and he knew it. He needed someone bigger and mightier than himself, so he cried out to God. In his weakness, King Asa prayed a prayer:

> *"Lord, there is no one besides you to help the mighty and those without strength. Help us, Lord, our God, for we depend on you, and in your name, we have come against*

this large army. Lord, you are our God. Do not let a mere
mortal hinder you."

2 Chronicles 14:11

We read in verse 12 that the Lord re-routed the Cushite army and they fled from the land of Judah. Asa pursued them and the Cushites were wiped out. That is quite an answer to prayer!

Interestingly, in Asa's prayer, he cries out to the God who helps both the mighty and those without strength. This is an acknowledgement that there are seasons when we live and lead out of strength, but there are also seasons when we find ourselves in a place of weakness. In both of these scenarios we can put our dependence on the Lord. Asa's prayer is powerful because it reminds us of our need for God.

We read later in 2 Chronicles 15 that Asa and the people of Judah dedicated themselves again to the Lord, to seek him with all their heart and all their soul, and because of this the Lord gives them rest from war. There was peace for thirty-five years of Asa's reign, but in the thirty-sixth year, King Baasha of Israel declared war against King Asa of Judah. Now something changes in Asa's response. This time, instead of going to God, Asa goes to another king for help. He strikes up a partnership with the king of Aram which he hopes will see Israel's army defeated.

Hanani, a prophet, comes to King Asa and calls it like he sees it:

"Because you depended on the king of Aram and have not
depended on the Lord your God, the army of the king of
Aram has escaped from you. Were not the Cushites and
Libyans a vast army with many chariots and horsemen?

When you depended on the Lord, he handed them over to you. For the eyes of the Lord roam throughout the earth to show himself strong for those who are wholeheartedly devoted to him. You have been foolish in this matter. Therefore, you will have wars from now on."

2 Chronicles 16:7-9 CSB

What happened to this king who had once cried out to God, totally dependent on him? What happened to this king who in his weakness trusted in the Lord for his strength? I can tell you what happened. Asa forgot he needed God. He moved from God-dependence to self-sufficiency. We can all fall into this trap. We cry out to God in our weakness but so often we forget him in our strength.

The Stronger We Get, The More We Need God

As our son's collarbone began to heal and the better he felt, the more careful he needed to be because his weakness became less obvious. Similarly, we need to understand that the stronger we feel, the more we need to press into God. Like King Asa, when our weaknesses become less obvious it can be so easy for us to forget our need for God. Asa began to rely not only on his *own* strength and might but also on his *own* resources and connections.

When we are mighty, we can make most things happen with our *own* finances, our *own* resources, and our *own* connections. This can be the bondage of wealth and power—it traps us in self-sufficiency. It's why Jesus taught in the New Testament that it is easier for a camel to go through the eye of a needle than for a rich man to enter the kingdom of heaven (Matthew 19:24). Friend, it is so important that you and I understand that the mightier we become the more we need God. The more successful, fruitful, healed, whole, favoured, rich, blessed and happy we become, the more necessary it is for us to press into God, lean on him, and keep him at the centre of our being. Here is why:

> *In the thirty-ninth year of his reign Asa developed a disease in his feet. His disease was severe, yet even in his illness he did not seek the Lord, but [relied only on] the physicians.*
>
> *2 Chronicles 16: 12 AMP*

At first, as I read this verse, I couldn't understand why, in his severe sickness, King Asa continued to forget God and relied only on others? In previous circumstances, he had experienced the breakthrough power of God—he knew God was able! Why not lean on God in this moment?

The answer? Pride. Without dependency, *might leads to pride.* Our pride keeps us from acknowledging that we are without strength. King David writes about this in Psalm 21:7:

> *"For the king trusts in the Lord. The unfailing love of the Most High will keep him from stumbling."*

A king's only hope is to submit to a greater king—King Jesus. Nobody on this earth is so great and mighty that they can bypass trusting the Lord and not stumble at one point or another. This is the truth—no earthly leader is exempt from the need to depend wholeheartedly on God.

This is also why Jesus said:

"I am the vine; you are the branches. The one who remains in me and I in him produces much fruit because you can do nothing without me."

John 15:5

As a branch connected to the vine, we begin to produce fruit—lots of lovely, delicious fruit. The temptation is to stand there with all our lovely fruit and think that we produced it. *Look how amazing I am with all this fruitfulness.* What we forget is that it is only because we are connected to the vine that fruit begins to grow. Without the vine, the branch is nothing.

The need for this dependence makes a consistent prayer life that much more important because it keeps us connected to the vine. Prayer brings me to my knees and reminds me that: It's God, not me, it's his strength, not mine, his provision, not mine, his sufficiency, not mine. The stronger I become, the more I need God.

My problem was I thought I knew that. I thought I *was* dependent because I was devoted. I prayed. I read my Bible. I even journaled—that's gotta count for something, right? But what I learnt from King Asa's prayer made me question whether that dependence is an automatic given or not.

Devotion Doesn't Always Mean Dependence

Asa is described as being wholeheartedly devoted throughout his entire life. It therefore seems to me that King Asa never lost his *devotion to* God, but he did lose his *dependence on*

God. Asa was devoted but he wasn't always dependent. How can someone be devoted to God in one breath and yet forget that they need him in the next? Perhaps it is because a lot of the time our devotion is often reflected in our *doing*. It focuses on the *what* of our relationship with God. Contrary to that, dependence is more reflected in our *being*—it focuses on the *who* of our relationship with God.

Think of Martha again. When she complained to Jesus that she was the only one doing all the work, Jesus praised Mary for choosing what was most important. Martha was devoted, but Mary was dependent. I don't think Jesus was saying that what Martha was doing wasn't valuable. I think that he was saying that just because we are devoted in our *doing*, it doesn't automatically transfer to dependence in our *being*. We can have a consistent prayer or devotional life but still not be brought to our knees in desperate need of God. Little did I know that within a few weeks of that New Year's Eve barbeque, I would enter my own season of utter helplessness. I, too, had to be brought to my knees—literally—before I could realise this powerful truth.

Ultimately, the lesson I was learning on this journey was to become *irresponsible*. God didn't just want my devotion—my doing of all the things and ticking all the boxes—he wanted my dependence. I had to start asking myself: *Am I devoted? Am I dependent? How can I be both?* It wasn't until I relinquished my need to control and be self-sufficient, that I began to experience not only healing and freedom coming to me, but fruitfulness in others around me. I think God's heart is that we would all make that shift from devotion to dependence, and even better, that we would live out of both of those places. And he doesn't want this just so that we can live lighter and less weighed down—he wants it because his greatest desire is that we live connected to him. Since the beginning of time, his heart has been that we wouldn't just *do* more for him, but that we would *be* with him more.

XIII
Handing Back Responsibility

M Y ELEVEN-YEAR-OLD WAS DANGLING UPSIDE DOWN SOME thirty metres above a concrete pad . . . and I was sure I was going to throw up. Our eldest son had gone to our local theme park to celebrate the end of the school year with his mates. A few of us parents tagged along for supervision, and after a handful of rides, the boys made their way to the *Stratosfear*.

This ride was all my nightmares wrapped up in one rollercoaster. It had two levels of intensity. The lower level was called 'less extreme', where the motion was back and forth, nothing too awful—just enough to make you want to bring up your breakfast. Then there was the higher intensity level, denoted 'very extreme'. Stepping foot on this ride was closer to a near-death experience than a fun leisure park ride. This thing swung from side to side, and as it did, it kept rising higher and higher until it reached the pinnacle, where its riders dangled upside down for about six of the longest seconds before being carried over, making a full 360-degree circle.

The *Stratosfear* was the ride the kids wanted to do, and all of them jumped on the lower-intensity one . . . all except my son, who jumped into the one that leaves you dangling thirty metres in the sky. Before I had a chance to rein him in, he was being strapped into the harness. Nothing could have prepared me for what it felt like to watch my skinny eleven-year-old make a 360-degree spin and hang upside down. I couldn't watch it. I wanted to be sick at the sight of it. I have never felt more relieved than when his feet hit the floor, and he was safe on solid ground.

I can't help but think that life can sometimes feel like we are dangling upside down, thirty metres above ground, holding on for dear life. It's like we unknowingly jumped into the 'very extreme' line, and now we feel spun in a full three-sixty, hanging on for what feels like a lifetime. We have no option but to close our eyes and hope that our feet hit solid ground soon. It is in those seasons that we learn about a trust in the Lord that goes way beyond any of our own understanding. It's the kind of trust that offers no other option but an all-in response—my feet are off the floor, and I am putting all my trust in the One who holds me. But it took my life being completely upended to teach me this.

Very Extreme Trust

The year 2020 was the hardest year of our married life, and the pandemic had nothing to do with it. We came home from our sabbatical overseas in February, ready to take on a new role—it was a new season with exciting challenges. Little did we know that the journey we were about to begin would have us clinging to our faith like never before. My husband developed a balance disorder while we were overseas, that was left undiagnosed for the better part of a year. The disorder caused vertigo, fatigue and headaches, among other symptoms. The physical challenges that accompanied this disorder evolved into severe panic attacks and anxiety—a stress response from the constant intense dizziness.

These significant health difficulties, both physical and mental, had us questioning if we could continue with life as we knew it or if we would be thrown off course altogether. After hitting rock bottom, we were desperate for help. Nine months on from his first dizzy episode, Steve eventually received a diagnosis for the balance and at a similar time was also diagnosed with several mental health issues: post-traumatic stress caused by the constant attacks of dizziness, complicated grief as he grieved the life he thought was about to get ripped away, and depression— he could no longer see any hope for the future. Usually, I was able to fix things—I was capable, I had the drive—but this time there was nothing I could do. I was utterly helpless.

If I didn't have a handle on what it meant to trust the Lord before, I was certainly about to find out now. We were upside down, thirty metres and more above ground, holding on for dear life, and praying for the ride to end. I'm sure you can imagine that, with my husband struggling just to get out of bed in the morning, my false responsibility habits had a field day. That's right! They went into overdrive! This scenario only solidified my damaging running commentary, making it easier for me to dig myself deeper into the hole of self-reliance and become that self-appointed hero. I set to work, once again, to carry everything.

Thankfully, our friends who happened to be counsellors, spent a bit of time with me over this season unpacking some of the emotions associated with being the caregiver for someone experiencing severe mental health challenges. It didn't take long for false responsibility to rear its head. After all, it was completely understandable that this particular season would confirm my belief that if I didn't do it all then everything would soon come crumbling down. My counsellor friends asked me the question, "If taking responsibility for everything can no longer play a role in your life, what new thing could be taken up in its place?" Without skipping a beat, I heard a whisper in my heart: *Trust.* As I listened, a picture formed in my mind of myself sitting back in an armchair—a big comfy armchair. I knew it was the Lord speaking to me about the new position that he was now inviting me to approach my life from.

It was a beautiful, tangible, and helpful picture of what trust really could look like in my life. *Trust looks like sitting back in a big comfy chair and watching God at work.* And this wasn't just a picture, it was an invitation. Trust was not *me* taking responsibility for everything and everyone. Trust was not *me* carrying the weight of the whole world for fear of what might happen if I didn't. Trust was not *me* stepping in to catch all the things that were teetering on the edge. Trust was me learning to sit in the truth and knowledge that God was not only at work and not only fully able to bear the weight—but that *he* was also ultimately responsible.

Trust is an Overflow

Do you have a friend who loves to name-drop? They just can't help themselves but tell you who that seemingly important or partially famous person is that they have some very stretched connection to. Why do people do this? Aside from it being incredibly annoying, it allows a person to borrow the reputation, fame, or stature of that famous 'friend' in such a way that it boosts their own reputation, fame, or stature.

Certain names give credibility. If someone else sends you somewhere exclusive or offers you their members-only discount, they often say, "Just give them my name" or "Just tell them I sent you." They are using their name to raise your credibility.

I would often visit my dad at his work for lunch, and if I turned up to the reception and gave them my first name alone, they would look at me blankly, but if I gave them my father's name, they would open the door and let me in, no questions asked. Why? Because his name carried weight: it gave me credibility not because of who I was but because of who he was. What was true for my earthly father is even more true for our heavenly Father. His name carries credibility.

I am going to be *that* annoying friend, and name-drop for a moment now. Do you know . . .

El Elyon, *The Most High God*
El-Roi, *The God Who Sees*
El Shaddai, *The Lord God Almighty*
Jehovah Jireh, *The Lord Will Provide*
Jehovah Nissi, *The Lord My Banner; He is Our Hope*

Jehovah-Raah, *The Lord My Shepherd*
Jehovah Rapha, *The Lord Who Heals*
Jehovah Shalom, *The Lord is Peace*
Jehovah Shammah, *The Lord is There*

God's name carries weight, and it gives credibility to his character. So, when I know his name, trust becomes an overflow—the overflow of simply knowing him. The Psalmist puts it like this:

> *Those who know your name trust in you, for you, Lord, have never forsaken those who seek you.*
>
> *Psalm 9:10*

Trust is far easier when I know the trustworthy character of the One I am depending upon.

It is in my darkest valleys that I have experienced the greatest revelation of who my God is. The most difficult seasons in life will reveal many of the different aspects of his character. As I draw nearer to him during those times, I learn more about who he is: I learn of his peace, his wisdom, his protection, and his provision. I learn of his faithfulness, his mercy, his comfort, and his grace. There are a multitude of facets to his character and they are all revealed through and by the different circumstances that we face in our lives, and yes, that includes the valleys.

The key is in the knowing. The only way to develop this trust is to spend time building a relationship with God so that we grow in our knowledge of who he is. Relationships are built through time, conversation, discovery, and appreciation. We uncover more of who he is when we prioritise opening the Word daily. We grow in our intimacy with him when we commit to developing a habit of constant conversation through prayer. Our eyes are opened to his character when we consistently surround ourselves with his creation, either in nature or in community.

The God Who is Able

Not only is it easy to trust the God you know, but it's even easier to trust him when you know him as *able*. Repeatedly, the Bible uses the phrase, "Now to him who is able . . ."

Now to him who is able to strengthen you.
Romans 16:25

Now to him who is able to protect you from stumbling and make you stand in his presence.
Jude 24

Now to him who is able to do above and beyond all that we ask or think.
Ephesians 3:20

The word 'able' in these scriptures comes from the Greek word *dynamai*, which means 'to be capable, strong, and powerful'. That adds fullness to the meaning, doesn't it? Now to him who is *capable*, to him who is *strong*, to him who is *powerful*—that's a God we can put our trust in.

News flash . . . it says, "Now to *him* who is able"—not, "Now to *me* who is able." And yet how often have I gone about my relationships, my struggles, raising my kids, and fulfilling my ministry call as though it is *me* who is able?

The year that followed our 'year from hell' was a big one. Within the first six months, we sold our home, bought a new house, and moved into it. I released my first book and we completed an enormous extension of our church building. Steve was getting better. A glimmer of light was peeping into our tunnel. Even so, it all felt incredibly overwhelming.

I can clearly remember three consecutive weekends in June of that year. On the first weekend we moved house, the next weekend we completed the church renovation and reopened the building with a big event, and on the third weekend we hosted our annual women's conference with six hundred women attending. In the midst of all this, I had a conversation with a fellow pastor that went like this: "Are we going to be able to pull this off?" I asked him, totally overwhelmed by the month that lay ahead. His response has remained with me to this day: "We have done all we can do, and we have given it our best. God will just have to do the rest. We really have no other choice."

He was right. Sometimes you can't do more, be more, give more, say more. Your only option is to take a step back, let God step in, and let him finish the work he began. We can do our very best but when it comes down to it the rest is up to God.

It reminds me of a story in 1 Kings 17, where we read of the prophet Elijah who, during a severe drought, comes to a particular town and meets a widow there who is gathering wood. He asks her to bring him some water . . . and a loaf of bread as well. She explains to him that she only has a small amount of flour and oil, just enough to make one loaf of bread.

It would be the last meal for her and her son before they had nothing left to eat.

The prophet replies, "No problem, before you make yours, make one for me." She does not have enough and yet he asks her to give more. That just doesn't add up, does it?

Let me show you how he encouraged her:

> For this is what the Lord God of Israel says, "The flour jar will not become empty and the oil jug will not run dry until the day the Lord sends rain on the surface of the land."
>
> 1 Kings 17:14

And that was exactly what happened. The flour did not run empty, the oil did not run dry. The whole household ate for many days.

I can only imagine the fear, anxiety and worry she must have been feeling as she poured out the flour and oil. It was an act of obedience that required her trust that God would do what only he could do. What a beautiful picture of a God who steps into our lack. A God who finishes the work he starts in and through us. A God who carries his purposes through to completion because *he is the God who is able.*

Understanding Our Part

Our God is trustworthy and able. We can leave our 'stuff' with him knowing he can carry it. That being said, we still do have a part to play—a portion of responsibility in our partnership with the Lord. As we believe for him to work in our lives, in our hopes, in our struggles, in our good times and hard times, we do have a job to do but it isn't as complicated or as weighty as we might think it is. It's quite simple really. Our part is the *Amen*.

Wait! What? Do you mean to tell me that our part is not to force, manipulate, or push to make things work, or to try and figure it out on our own? Correct—our part is the "Amen," the "I agree, Lord", the "Yes, Lord, let it be so."

2 Corinthians 1:20 says:

> *For all of God's promises have been fulfilled in Christ with a resounding "Yes!" And through Christ, our "Amen" (which means "Yes") ascends to God for his glory.*

We can often become so desperate for the fulfilment of something—a prayer, a promise, an outcome—that we take on what is not our responsibility. We make the result and the fulfilment our job. But our job is not the result; that's the job of the One who is able. There is a difference between what is our responsibility and what is God's responsibility. Our responsibility is the asking and the amen, his responsibility is the answer. Our responsibility is obedience, his responsibility is the outcome. Our responsibility is the seeking, his responsibility is the revelation.

In the book of John chapter 6, the crowds had searched and found Jesus and his disciples at Capernaum. When they reached him, this was what he said to them:

> *"I tell you the truth, you want to be with me because I fed you, not because you understood the miraculous signs.*

But don't be so concerned about perishable things like food. Spend your energy seeking the eternal life that the Son of Man can give you. For God the Father has given me the seal of his approval."

They replied, "We want to perform God's works, too. What should we do?"

Jesus told them, "This is the only work God wants from you: Believe in the one he has sent."
John 6:26-29

Jesus is trying to encourage these people to do only what is their responsibility—to believe in the One sent by God. When they desired to do great things, perform miracles, and be part of something bigger for God, their instinct was to work for it themselves. But the response from Jesus is contrary to that, and I believe he would say the same to you and me today: "The only work God wants from you, is to believe."

Fulfilling our part means resisting the urge to work for that which only God can do. It means letting go of the false responsibility that I have assigned myself to fix, force, carry, create, hold, make, solve, and sort everything.

BACK NOW, TO OUR MAMMOTH SIX MONTHS. IT WAS JUNE, AND WE had come to the final event of our women's conference. I was standing in our new board room overlooking the café, watching as hundreds of women filled the space, connecting and laughing. As I watched, I noticed something surprising about myself—I was at rest. The overwhelming feeling I had in that moment was not stress or busyness. I was not feeling panic or even exhaustion. Instead, the feeling was gratitude. It was as if I was finally living in the "unforced rhythms of grace" I had longed for (Matthew 11:29 MSG). The words from my colleague a few weeks prior came back to me: "God will do the rest." And he did. I realised at that moment I wasn't just standing overlooking our cafe, I was sitting back in my big, comfy seat of trust, watching God at work.

Once I began to live my life from my position in that seat of trust, it was like a weight had been lifted. Interestingly, nothing about my physical or surrounding circumstances had changed. I still felt busy and often stressed at times, but slowly, the crushing weight of false responsibility I had become so familiar with began to lift. It felt strange and out of the ordinary for me, and it took me a while to put words to it. I felt light. I felt carried. I felt like I was living the words of Jesus: "Take my yoke upon you . . . and you will find rest for your souls" (Matthew 11:29).

Let me ask you: Are there responsibilities or burdens you've been carrying, that you know you need to entrust to God? Thinking about those things, how would it feel to be able to sit back in the big comfy seat of trust and watch God at work?

Could it be that within the busyness and pressure of your life right now, God is inviting you to a new seat? I believe he offers that invitation to each one of us. Even when it might feel like terrible timing to be sitting down, perhaps it is the best timing of all. It is only when we have to lean on him and trust that we see just how *able* our God is.

XIV

Saying No (Without the Guilt)

THE WORDS, *GUILTY, GUILTY, GUILTY,* PLAY OVER AND OVER IN MY mind, taunting me as I lie awake in bed at night! *Did I do all that I could? Should I have said it differently? Did I come across too harshly? Was it okay that I couldn't be there?* I know I am not the only one who plays re-runs of their day, the conversations and the interactions, right before they drift off to sleep at night. The 'should haves' and 'could haves', the second-guessing and the weighing up of words spoken—all fighting for attention.

Guilt. We feel it, don't we? The worry about feeling guilty is one of the things that stops me from making decisions about my commitments that I know I really should be making. Decisions that—under a microscope—no one would question or begrudge me for, no one would think anything of, and yet I just can't kick the feelings of guilt.

Guilt for not choosing to help.

Guilt for asking someone else to take it on.

Guilt for saying no.

Guilt for prioritising myself or my family.

Guilt for deliberately making myself unavailable.

Mental health coach and writer, Darius Cikanavicius, says this of the hyper-responsible individual: ". . . the person tends to take on unjust responsibility and feels overly guilty if things around them go wrong."[7]

Guilt. But what about grace?

I was reading my Bible one morning, as I have developed the habit of doing each day, when I came to a passage that hit me in a way it hadn't before. It spoke to me right where I was at. It came like a gift. It was full of God's grace. He had seen the internal tension I was battling, and he came gently and beautifully and gave me what felt like a 'get out of jail free' card.

At the beginning of Matthew chapter 14, John the Baptist has been beheaded. The news reaches Jesus and, no doubt in grief, he withdraws to a remote place to be alone with the Father. But the crowds follow him. A large crowd gathers, so Jesus attends to them. He heals the sick and miraculously feeds five thousand people. Then we read:

> *Immediately* **he made the disciples get into the boat and go ahead of him** *to the other side, while he dismissed the crowds. After dismissing the crowds,* **he went up on**

7 www./psychcentral.com/blog/psychology-self/2018/11/guilt-responsibility-dysfunction#1

the mountain by himself to pray. Well into the night he was there alone. Meanwhile, the boat was already some distance from the land, battered by the waves because the wind was against them ...

Matthew 14:22-24

It gave so much relief to my guilt-ridden heart to read about a moment when Jesus sent his disciples away so he could be alone. He made them move on without him. He made them leave him on his own. He even sent them off in such a way that they had no way of following him. They would have had to jump out of a moving boat to reach him. He needed the time without them. And we all need to listen to these words: *It was okay that he did this.*

I wonder how many of them wanted to stay with him. I wonder how many of them would have insisted that they stay and help with the crowds. I wonder how many offered to keep him company. Jesus forced time and space between himself and those he led and loved. And get this—he did it knowing they were going to face some wild weather. That's right, Jesus sends them all away and heads up the mountain to be on his own. Meanwhile, back in the boat without him, his friends find themselves in a storm.

Jesus put distance between himself and the people he led, even when they were facing trouble. He was away long enough for them to sail out far away from dry land and find themselves caught up in a raging storm. When morning came—and note that he left them all night in that storm—only then did Jesus go and appear to them on the water. Eventually, he gets into the boat with the disciples, and the wind stops.

Okay, breaking news: I am not Jesus. I can't rescue anyone from a storm and I can't walk on water. I can't fix everything for everyone. And yet, if Jesus—who *can* rescue people from storms, walk on water, and fix everything for everyone— prioritises time out from those he leads, then I should certainly feel permission to do the same. By the way, the same is true for you, friend. This revelation was eye-opening, life-changing, and mind-blowing all at the same time. It instantly gave me peace in my heart. Through the example of Jesus, you and I have permission to create space, and if need be, force distance. It enables and empowers us to say no. Jesus demonstrates to us boundaries at their finest!

Often, we feel guilty for giving attention to our own needs. This was so true for me, but more than that, I discovered I had lost touch with what my own needs were. The first step in getting back in touch was being able to see that I had needs. I remember when I was asked the question, "What is it that you need?" If you could have listened into my brain at that moment, you would have heard the whistling of the wind because honestly, there was not a lot going on in there. My mind was drawing a blank and I could not even articulate what my needs might have been.

It took someone showing me a series of words on paper for me to be able to recognise my own needs in them. Words like: acknowledgement, reassurance, appreciation, and dependability. Needs like: creativity, nurture, peace, and protection. If we can put words to our needs, it is far easier for us to acknowledge them. I found that even just giving words to them in a way that helped me to voice them, was half the battle already won. Simply saying them out loud helped me deal with the otherwise relentless guilt more than I could have imagined.

A few chapters before Jesus sends his disciples away, he gives them advice for times when they will be faced with guilt—or more likely, with fear and worry about how other people might respond. In Matthew 10, Jesus sends them out to minister, saying:

> *"If anyone is unworthy, let your peace return to you. If anyone does not welcome you, or listen to your words, shake the dust off your feet when you leave that house or town."*
>
> Matthew 10:12-14

Now, I understand that the context of this passage is about rejection of the disciples' ministry and the message they carried, but it also gives us some insight as to how we can respond in the face of other people's opinions, reactions, and disappointments. It provides us with an image of what it looks like to *not* allow people's opinions and comments to niggle away and cause us to feel guilt and shame. When we lie awake at night worrying about what someone might think if we do this, or don't do that, then we have allowed those things to steal our peace. But Jesus is saying that when we leave that person or situation, we can take our peace with us. I realised that what Jesus was encouraging his disciples to do in their situation, I too can do. I can 'shake the dust off' whatever situation I'm feeling guilty about and keep my peace.

Choosing to *care less* doesn't mean that I don't care at all. I always found myself feeling seriously guilty because I thought that not making myself available to people meant that I don't care. But I do care, it's just that I have to choose to care less about certain things than I do about other things—we all do. Saying yes to one thing always means you will have to say no to something else. That's just good mathematics, otherwise, it doesn't all add up.

Re-designing your life so that you can be free from the trap of false responsibility means figuring out what you are willing to say no to. Sometimes caring less really is the best thing you can do—and believe it or not, things will still turn out just fine.

XV

Re-learning
to Rest

P ICTURE THREE BEADY EYES AND TWO SNOUTS STICKING OUT FROM beneath a gate. Those belong to our two delightful dogs— one of which has only one eye (if you're wondering). They like to sit at the front window or gate and bark at every car, every person, every dog, every cat, every bird, every leaf that passes by. Good luck to anyone in or near my home who is trying to get an afternoon nap—because they won't let you rest.

It often feels the same way with life, doesn't it? It never lets you rest! To the hyper-responsible, rest seems like a pipedream. You are already trying to keep your home at a reasonable standard of cleanliness, maintain healthy relationships with family and friends, and keep a healthy diet and lifestyle. You are trying to keep up with your workload, and also with your appearances on social media—the Lord knows if you didn't post about it, then it didn't happen. You might have kids—that's a job in itself, raising well-rounded humans—and on top of that, you've got pets to keep alive! I mean, rest? When do we fit that in?

I know exactly what it feels like to crave a moment's rest. Yet when it comes to God, rest is part of the deal. Look at what the psalmist writes:

> *The Lord is my shepherd; I have all that I need. He lets me rest in green meadows; he leads me beside peaceful streams. He renews my strength.*
>
> Psalm 23:1-3

When it says, "I have all that I need," that includes rest. Rest isn't a luxury. It's not extravagant to take a break. Rest is a *need*. And God provides our needs. His intention is for us to rest, to lie down, and to be restored.

How can we get the rest we need? Only in the knowledge of who he is and under the confidence of his provision.

I have all that I need. This is the context in which he invites us to rest. Here's what this psalm tells me: I can rest today because I am secure in my tomorrow.

I once read a fascinating story. In their book, *Sleeping with Bread,* Dennis Linn writes about an orphanage that had received a group of children who had lost their parents during a war. Every night, the children struggled to sleep. Many could not fall asleep, and even if they did, they would often wake fearful in the night. The carers tried many things to help these children sleep, yet nothing worked—until they noticed one child grasping a piece of bread as he slept. That gave them an idea. What if they tried giving each child a piece of bread to put under their pillow while they slept? Interestingly, this worked! If they had a piece of bread under their pillow, every child slept soundly from the moment they went to bed until morning. Why? Because with the bread under their pillow, they knew where their next meal was coming from. They slept soundly knowing the need that mattered most to them was provided. [8]

Provision for Rest

For a lot of us, rest has become our most basic need. We can hardly imagine lying down and feeling utterly relaxed. Yet the phrase "He makes me lie down . . ." is referencing exactly that. A sprawling out, mouth open, drool-dripping kind of rest. It is the kind of rest that takes place when one is completely at ease. When we know the Lord as our Shepherd and we know that in him we have all that we need, we can confidently and securely rest in the knowledge that not only is my today in his hands, but my tomorrow is also secured. Perhaps you need to hear this today: *You can rest.* God has made provision for you to do so.

In Exodus 16 we read about the season that followed the Israelites' time of slavery in Egypt. Remember that the Israelites were used to being slaves—their 'normal' was working and never resting—there was no such thing as work-life balance. Understandably, this was a hard adjustment for them. They'd never experienced a Sabbath. They'd never known a rest that didn't come at great cost. But God wanted them to know they could rest in him and *still have all they needed.*

> *The Lord said to Moses, "I am going to rain bread from heaven for you. The people are to go out each day and gather enough for that day."*
>
> *Exodus 16:4*

---

8 Paraphrased from *Sleeping with Bread* by Dennis Linn, Paulist Press, 1995.

This feels like a lesson in trust to me. Did they trust that God was going to provide *every* day or just this once? Did they feel the need to hoard to make sure they had enough, or could they live trusting God's supply would be fresh with each new day?

> *So the Israelites did this. Some gathered a lot, some a little. When they measured by quarts, the person who gathered a lot had no surplus and the person who gathered a little had no shortage. Each gathered as much as he needed to eat.*
>
> *Exodus 16:17-18*

What a wonderful picture of tailor-made provision! Regardless of the need, however big or small, God knows it and he provides. This is what the psalmist is trying to say in Psalm 23. He is our Shepherd; therefore, we want for nothing. God is responsible for providing all our needs.

But then God digs deeper:

> *"Understand that the Lord has given you the sabbath; therefore on the sixth day he will give you two days worth of bread. Each of you will stay where you are; no one is to leave this place on the seventh day."*
>
> *Exodus 16:29*

God is teaching his people to rest. He is not only saying you have to rest. He's saying, "I'm going to provide enough so that you *can* rest. I'm going to provide on the days you work—but also on the days you don't."

The same is true for us. God knows that our natural tendency is to strive, to be busy, to push and try to make it on our own. It's the 'self-made man' mentality, but we forget that everything we have has come from God in the first place. We're not self-made people at all. Ironically, just as with the Israelites, it's often in our rest that God gives us what we really need. We don't have to fret about what might be lost if we stop. We don't have to worry about what might not be happening or what we might not have if we were to rest. He provides so that we can rest. He doubles down on provision to sustain us through our seasons of rest.

Stations and Stages of Rest

The Hebrew word for 'leads' in Psalm 23 means 'to journey by stations or stages'. This gives us some clues as to the way the Lord, as our Shepherd, invites us to rest. God is constantly inviting us to rest as we journey with him throughout our lives.

If you have ever run a long-distance race, you would know that the course is punctuated along the way with refuge or refuelling stations. At every station, there are water bottles and electrolyte drinks, oranges or other energy sources; there are bathrooms, first aid, and—possibly the most important—encouragement. Each station provides the refreshment and the fuel you need to carry you through to the next station. It's helpful for a runner's mindset, to know that they don't have to get all the way to the end; they just have to reach the next refuge station.

Resting in stages or stations is God's design for us too. It's the way he intended for us to live. And just as in the marathon race, his expectation is not that we would run without refuelling. At each stage or station, he offers us everything we need to carry us through to the next. He does this in four ways: in seasons, celebrations, sabbaths, and sleep.

1. Seasons

The author of Ecclesiastes tells us, "For everything there is a season, a time for every activity under heaven" (Ecclesiastes 3:1). This is the way God designed the world. We have spring, summer, autumn, and winter. We have one year followed by another. We have expressions like, "This season is coming to an end" or "I am entering into a new season." In giving us these naturally occurring breaks, God is inviting us to rest—to honour the change in season. The end of a season and the beginning of the next is an opportunity to pause, reflect, and be thankful. It's a chance to recognise what's gone before us and be hopeful for what lies ahead. It is an invitation to rest.

We all have obvious seasons, like a Christmas break or summer holidays. But there are also shifts in life's seasons, such as when a child finishes primary or secondary school, or when you move from one job to another. We're often quick to move through these shifts, but at what cost? I wonder if somewhere in your life now, or perhaps coming up soon, there is an opportunity to pause for a moment and invite God's rest before you jump into the next season.

2. Celebrations

As well as marking the seasons, it is so important that in the busyness of our lives, we don't miss out on the opportunity—and the invitation from the Lord—to stop and have a *praise party* every now and then. We have natural moments in our Christian calendar that allow for this; times like Easter, Christmas, and Pentecost. But we can also do this on a more individual scale: birthdays, achievements, new jobs, babies and anniversaries.

We need to make the most of these moments. They force us to take a break from our everyday lives and pressures.

Throughout Scripture, we find numerous festivals and celebrations: the Feast of Passover, the Feast of Unleavened Bread, the Feast of Firstfruits, the Feast of the Harvest, the Feast of Trumpets, the Day of Atonement and the Feast of Tabernacles. Interestingly, these festivals and celebrations are also connected with rest. In them we see God inviting his people to cease their normal work-life routine to acknowledge the lordship, provision, and sovereignty of God. These were times of rest, but also of celebration, times for remembering and for glorifying the goodness of God.

James 1:17 reminds us that every good and perfect gift is from above. When we celebrate, we are simply making a point of stopping the pattern of our normal life's rhythm to acknowledge God's goodness to us.

3. Sabbath

In providing enough manna for both the sixth and the seventh day, God taught his people about the *need* for rest long before he gave the *commandment* to rest. In other words, the precedent comes before the command. God was teaching a nation who were once slaves, but were now free, what it meant to cease work—and he assured them of his provision in doing so. Then he said, "Okay, let's set this in stone and make it a regular thing."

"Remember the Sabbath day, to keep it holy: You are to labor six days and do all your work, but the seventh day

is a Sabbath to the Lord your God. You must not do any work—you, your son or daughter, your male or female servant, your livestock, or the resident alien who is within your city gates. For the Lord made the heavens and the earth, the sea, and everything in them in six days; then he rested on the seventh day. Therefore, the Lord blessed the Sabbath day and declared it holy."

Exodus 20:8 -11

God knows that if we are to be continually refreshed and renewed in the way that is necessary for us, we need more than seasonal rest and festival rejuvenation. He knows that on one day every week, we need to stop, reset, and refuel. The sabbath is God's pattern for living that began and was modelled by him at Creation when he worked six days and rested one. God is leading each of us to do the same. We are called to punctuate our working week with a day of rest. Your body needs it. Your emotions need it. Your soul and your spirit need it.

It has been so hard for me to learn how to do 'rest'. Little Miss "I'm okay, I've got this" had to learn how to permit herself to rest. To do this, I had to understand that it is God who commanded this as his best for me—and it's God's best for you. It isn't always easy though, is it? Sometimes setting aside an entire day simply isn't possible.

I find that it is important that I plan everything else, so that 'rest' happens. If I don't, it won't happen—other things will take priority, and I will always find some excuse not to stop. I have chosen to redirect my entire week so that it leads to rest. I don't leave it to chance. I schedule my to-dos, assigning them to particular days and ensuring that I get them done, leaving my sabbath day free. I prioritise the most important things, giving them the greatest amount of my attention during my workdays. Whatever I don't get done, I push to the next week. By writing down those 'next week' tasks, I free up the mental space I would normally spend worrying about what I have and haven't done.

Let's be realistic though—it is often not work that keeps us from rest, it's home. Life-admin, laundry, dishes, cleaning—it's never-ending! I don't always get the balance right, but I do attempt to do whatever I can in my weekday routines to ensure that if for one day I don't do any housework, our home will not go into a nuclear meltdown.

For me, a day of rest might look like sleeping in, taking the morning slowly, reading a book, or taking the dog for a walk—it's a family day. A day to reconnect, refresh, and refuel. I do whatever fills my cup.

And if all my best intentions and planning fail, I have learnt to still be kind to myself—five minutes of rest is better than none, starting small is still a start, and doing just one thing for myself is better than doing nothing at all. If you aren't ensuring that you at least attempt to cease all work and rest on one day a week, can I suggest you start now and begin planning for a weekly sabbath?

4. Sleep

God not only created a weekly pattern of rest on the Sabbath but he also created a twenty-four-hour cycle of day and night. He gave us the day and he gave us the night. In this, He has given us an opportunity for daily renewal.

His mercies are new every morning! But morning follows nighttime, and nighttime is for sleeping. Our bodies need rest, not just yearly, not just weekly, but *daily!* My husband's old running coach taught him that the body adapts and grows, not during activity, but during rest. Activity creates stress and load on your body, but it's the rest between the activity where you adapt to the stress and become stronger and fitter.

Good sleep is so important. Turn off your phone. Log off your emails. Switch off from work mode, chore mode, and to-do mode. When the day comes to an end, welcome the opportunity that the Lord has given us to rest.

Have More Fun

I realised at the age of thirty-six that somewhere along the way, I had forgotten how to have fun. We were staying with my aunt and uncle during a trip back home to the United Kingdom, when I found myself worrying about all sorts of things: Were the kids being too noisy? Were they using their manners? Were they making a mess or being an irritation to our hosts? But each time I went to tell the boys to 'be quiet' or 'clean up' or 'stop that' my lovely aunty would just giggle and join the boys in their mischievous antics. In some of their antics that I thought would bring disapproval, she always found a way to celebrate them instead. She taught me that it was okay to have more fun—that we could do well to laugh more. Being with her was a beautiful reminder to relax and to lean into the spontaneous joys of life.

After our stay with my fun aunty, we flew to Florida, where we headed straight to Disney World. Now my normal response in a theme park is to sit on the sidelines and let the kids go for it. I'd cheer them on and relish their enjoyment, but the rides were never my thing. But with our new mission to have fun, I knew that when it was time to hit the park I would need to throw myself all in. So, I did! I got the T-shirt and the Minnie ears, and I lined up with the boys for all the rides, even the scary and sickly ones. And let me tell you, we had all kinds of fun and created memories I know my boys will never forget!

Having more fun has become an essential part of my journey. It helps me rediscover and possess the joy of life over and over again. If there was one thing I had lost and now realised I wanted back, it was joy. And with each deliberate step that I took—the submission, the dependence, the trust and surrender, the new narrative, the rest and the embracing of spontaneity—I stepped closer and closer toward the life of rest I knew God intended for me.

XVI
Bringing Back Margin

A WARM BREEZE WAS BLOWING GENTLY THROUGH THE PALM TREES around the pool, the sun was shining, and we were in tropical Fiji celebrating both my dad's and Steve's significant birthdays. Our trip was nearly at an end, and after a week of enjoying doing next to nothing, we had decided to travel to an island resort for the day—to continue doing next to nothing. In the middle of the resort was a swimming pool that had two depths: the shallow ledge was waist-deep and quickly dropped off to a much deeper 1.8 metres—well above my head! At some stage in our resort day, I was sitting on a sun lounger reading a book. My dad was doing the same on the lounger next to me. The rest of the family was on the beach throwing a ball around. Five or six other resort guests were sitting around the pool, and a father and his little girl, probably toddler-age, were playing on the shallow ledge. For once, I was completely relaxed, soaking up the last moments of our time away—sun out, sun hat and glasses on, feet up with ice cream in hand.

Suddenly, out of the corner of my eye, I noticed my dad trying, with some difficulty, to get himself up out of his lounger. While propping himself up, he began pointing toward the swimming pool. My eyes scanned around to find what Dad was trying to bring to my attention. Sure enough, the toddler, who had just a few moments earlier been playing happily with her dad, was sinking toward the bottom of the deep end while her father was flailing around next to her struggling to stay afloat. It took me a split second to register that they were both in trouble. I could hear a faint and muffled "Help!" as he gasped for air.

Someone had to go in and help these people. By this time, the little girl had been under for a long time—too long. I put down my book and set my ice cream down carefully. It's strange the things that go through your mind when in a state of emergency—I distinctly remember not wanting to waste my ice cream by throwing it away carelessly. I threw off the sundress I was wearing over my swimming togs, tossed my hat aside and dived into the pool, sunglasses and sandals still on. I went straight for the little girl. Grabbing hold and pulling her upward, I swam her to the edge. Dad was waiting there for us and he immediately lifted her out of the water. I paused to see if she was breathing—miraculously, she was fine. I let out a sigh of relief. Thank God she was okay. At that same moment, I remembered the man! He was still struggling in the water! I turned back to find him, and with all my might—he wasn't a small fellow—I heaved him onto the shallow ledge where he could find his feet. Checking he was okay, I climbed out of the pool and headed back to my lounger . . . and to my waiting ice cream.

I look back on that day often. This scene could have ended very differently. It could have ended in tragedy. I feel thankful that I was there. But not just 'there'— I am thankful that I was *available and able* to jump in at that crucial moment to help. One thing I was acutely aware of the entire time was that I wouldn't have been able to save the father and his daughter if I'd been going under myself. If I had also been drowning, I would not have been any use to anyone.

I had the capacity and capability to swim them to safety when their lives depended on it, only because my own life did not depend on it. That reflection, from a poolside lounger on a tropical island, was not limited to a physical near-drowning. I knew the same truth applied to my real everyday life.

I remember when my life was pushed out to the limits. I knew the feeling of living in a big field right next to a cliff without fences. Back then, there was nothing standing between me and the edge, and I constantly felt like everything was about to topple over.

Living our lives without fences means we push everything out to the limit. We live tired, stressed, and under pressure, with our capacity always at maximum and only demanding more. Too many of us lack margin. The problem of living without margin is that there is no space between us and the edge of the cliff. And we need that space because without it any unexpected thing could send us hurtling directly over and onto the rocks below. That kind of maxed-out living leaves no contingency for emergencies, no reserves, and nothing left in the tank should we need it for the unexpected. If my poolside rescue has taught me anything, it's that life is full of the unexpected.

The Badge of Busyness

In our modern, fast-paced world, busyness is one of our greatest downfalls. We wear it like a badge of honour, as though busyness indicates our importance. I don't know if I can go one day without hearing, "Oh, I have been so busy!" in response to a simple, "How are you?" We just can't help ourselves, can we? We feel this need to fill our days with more, meaning slow days are never allowed to stay slow—we insist on filling the space in the same way we have to fill the silence of an awkward pause.

I wonder why we pride ourselves on being so busy. It could be that we like to be productive and feel as though we have accomplished something. It could be that we don't want to waste a minute of the life we have been given. Maybe we've just got used to being endlessly active. It could be any of those things, but it most likely stems from somewhere a little deeper. I know for me, busyness was just a coverup because I hadn't yet learnt that my value was not in my *doing*—somewhere deep inside I still thought I had to work to prove my worth. I have spent a lifetime seeking love, belonging, and 'okay-ness' in *doing* rather than *being*.

When working on a ruthless decluttering of our home, we often ask, "Do I still use this?" to determine whether or not we will hold onto an item. It's probably no surprise that if the answer is no then we get rid of it. When we think about our own usefulness, we often wrongly apply that same principle and think we will end up in a box in the attic if we are not productive every minute of the day.

It's considered a sign of good leadership to raise other leaders to the point where we can do ourselves out of a job. But that may also be why we hold onto doing all the things for longer than we should because we worry about where it leaves us. It speaks to an insecurity in us that without the 'busy badge', people may not need us and may turn their attention to someone who is doing something better, bigger and busier than us. We risk being overlooked and forgotten.

We keep ourselves sufficiently busy, busy, busy . . . and we become multi-tasking jugglers who fill our lives to the absolute brim, dancing way too close to the limit of our capacity, with the threat of losing it all constantly looming over us. And all the while, we become less and less available to the people who need us most.

Building Fences

Imagine with me what it might look like to build a fence along the unfenced side of our field. Instead of building the fence on the extreme edge of the cliff, let's build it twenty to thirty paces back from the cliff. Now there is plenty of space between the fence line and the crumbling cliff edge. Life inside the fence line begins to feel balanced and calm. We're living, not *at* our limits, but *within* our limits. Now we have the capacity to cope and the space to breathe, even when the unexpected hits, because we're not right on the edge—our life isn't crammed full. That sounds pretty wonderful, doesn't it? There's a lot of relief in living within a sensible boundary instead of up against the outer perimeter.

To shift the fence line and begin living with 'margin', we might need to ask ourselves some difficult questions. I find these helpful when it comes to making manageable and practical adjustments in my life:

1. What am I doing currently that is draining me? What activities or relationships leave me feeling empty?
2. What can I start doing that fills my cup?
3. What can I do regularly to keep my margin generous? Could I:
   - set an earlier bedtime?
   - limit screen time, especially before bed?
   - schedule time alone or time for myself?
   - spend more time having fun, relaxing, and laughing?
   - prioritise more regular time with God?
   - get out in the fresh air more?
   - start having a weekly sabbath?
4. What am I currently saying yes to that I should be saying no to?

Bringing back margin and building new fence lines is a deliberate task that requires us to be constantly mindful. Think of it like this: For everything you say no to, you get to say yes to something else. That might be yes to a day doing some of the things that you love but never have time to do. It might mean saying yes to picking up a new hobby, heading to the beach with a book, or taking your child for a milkshake. Just make sure your yes is tank-filling. I'm not saying it is easy, but it will be worth it.

> *Jesus said, "Come to me, all of you who are weary and carry heavy burdens, and I will give you rest. Take my yoke upon you. Let me teach you, because I am humble and gentle at heart, and you will find rest for your souls. For my yoke is easy to bear, and the burden I give you is light."*
>
> *Matthew 11:28-30*

I have learnt that living free from false responsibility is not just about creating margins and having boundaries, it's about changing the inner story we tell ourselves.

We are not responsible for everything.

Acknowledgements

There were many times along the way to writing this book when I wondered whether I could bring it to completion. It has been a two-year process of writing, editing, rewriting, more editing and writing some more. For seasons, I wrote every day. I wrote on days when I wanted to and days when I didn't want to. I wrote when I felt inspired, and I wrote when I was empty of creativity. I wrote at my desk, in my car, from my bed, in hotel rooms, in the kitchen, and at the beach. This was not a solitary journey. There were many people along the way who championed, cheered and mentored me through. I am so grateful to each of you.

Thank you, Steve, my amazing husband who is always the first person to say, "Do it, babe". You backed me from the beginning and said yes to the dream each time I asked something of you. You were in it with me, from building me a study nook in our spare room to carrying the cost of Author School and editing mentoring sessions. Thank you for the times you took care of things so that I could lock myself away and write.

Thank you to my incredible editor, publisher and now friend, Anya McKee, and the team at Torn Curtain Publishing. Anya, you dove headfirst into this book and invested hours into making it what it is today. Thank you for believing in and carrying it with me. I am so grateful for the way you gently brought out the best in me. Nobody gives ruthless feedback as sweetly as you. I appreciate you so much.

Thank you to my Author School writing group. We were a group of strangers from such different worlds, but we fast became one another's biggest cheerleaders. Weeks and weeks of writing, feedback, lectures and workshops but the highlight of it all was meeting in person at Laguna Beach in 2024. Keep writing, friends. The world needs your stories.

Thank you to our friends Mike and Liz. I don't have the words to thank you for the way you picked us up off the floor and helped us walk again. So much of this book has come out of the wisdom you shared with me. So many revelations sitting on couches unpacking life with you. Thank you is not enough but it's a start.

Thank you to my church family. Thank you for inviting us into your lives to pray for you, pastor you, lead you and champion you. We know we would not be where we are today without our loving church.

Thank you to our church oversight for your continued support and prayer for me and my family. Thank you for always pushing me to step into the calling that God has for my life and encouraging me as I do. I am grateful for every opportunity to minister, grow and become all God has called me to be.

To my family, friends and our staff team at Elim Christian Centre. I love you all so much. Your love and support has meant the world to me.

Lastly, my thanks goes to my Saviour and King, Jesus. I am who I am and do what I do because of your grace. I will never take for granted the privilege that it is to speak into the lives of others. Thank you for choosing me and allowing me to be part of your plan for the world.

About the Author

To hear more from Becs or to invite her to speak at your church or ministry event, please visit:

www.becsgreen.com